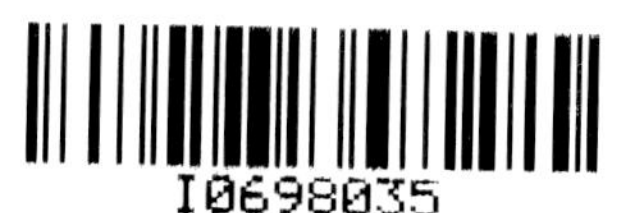

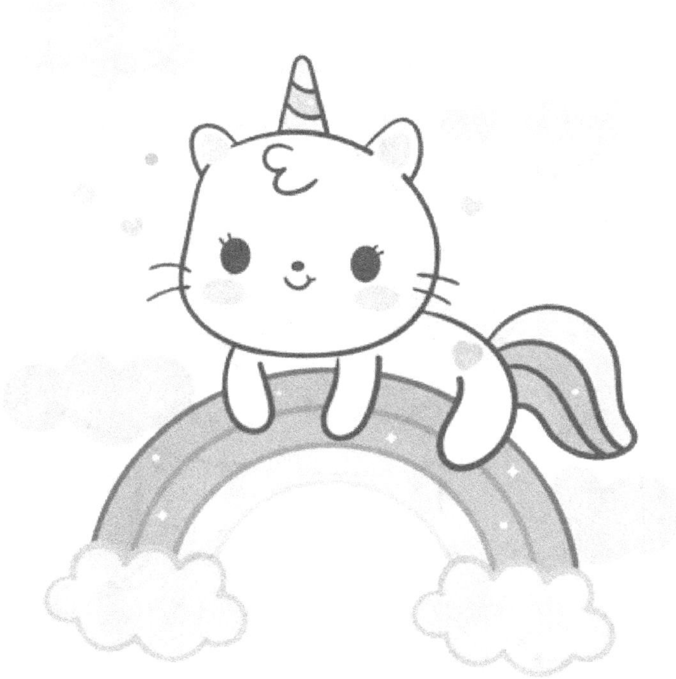

YOU'RE A REALLY PAW-SOME FRIEND!

Happy International Friendship Day!

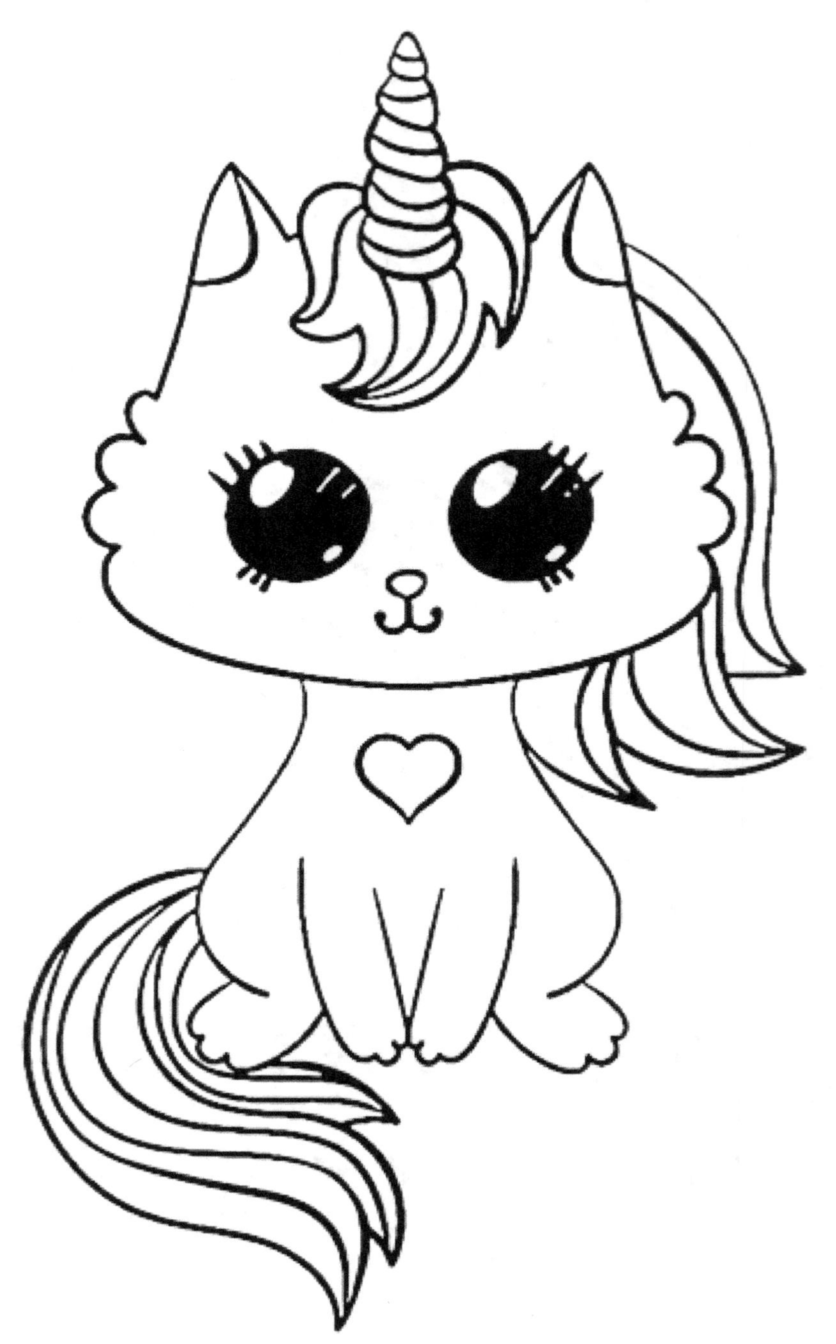

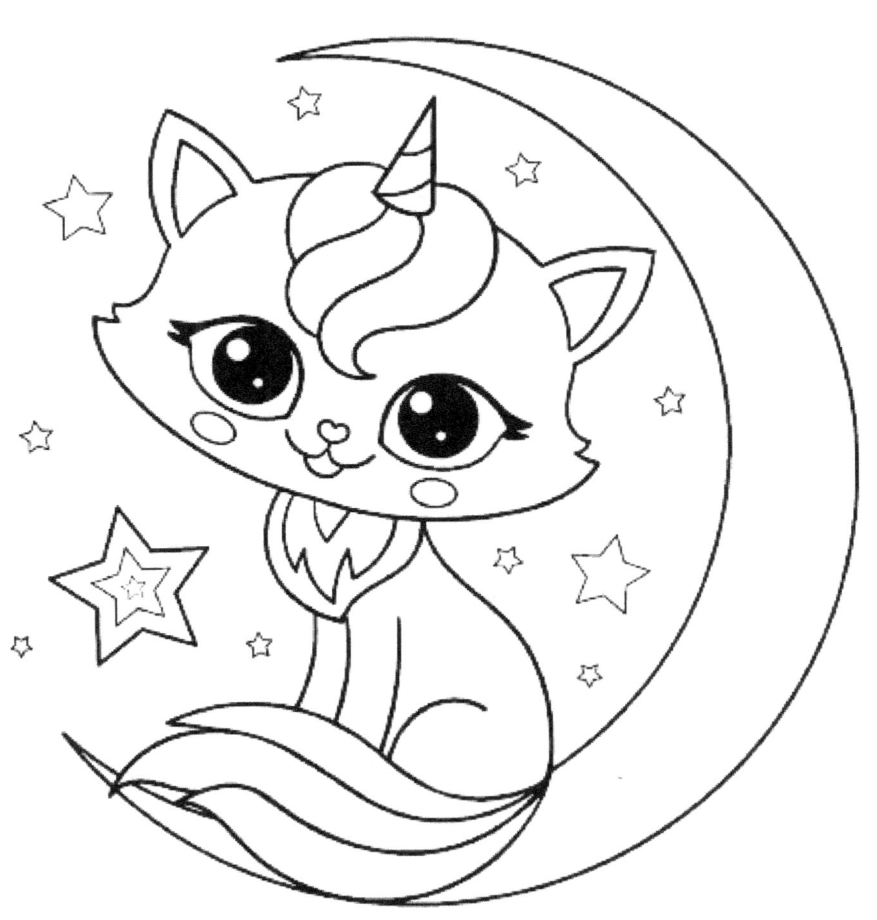

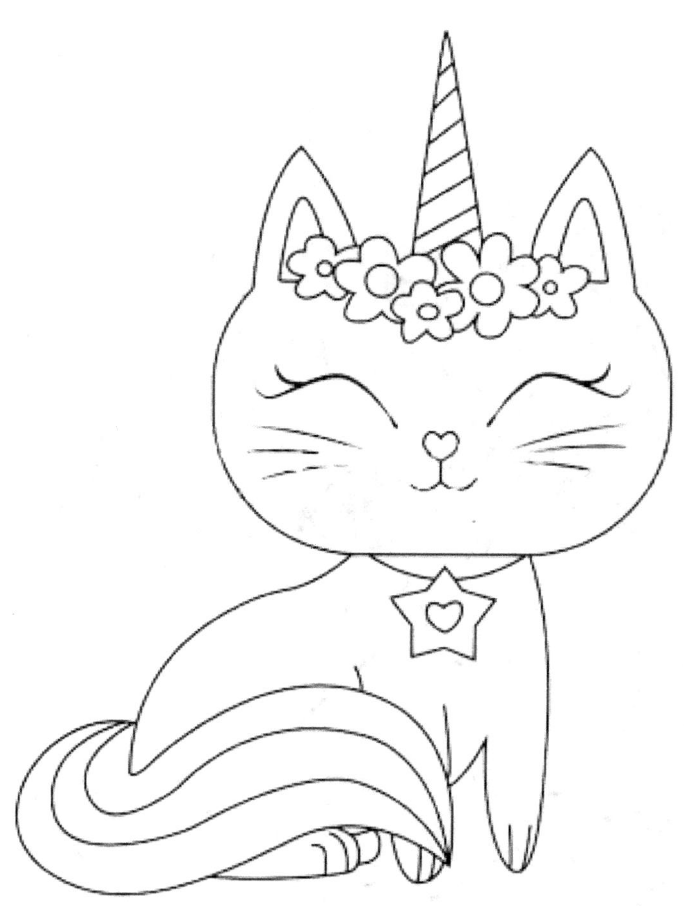

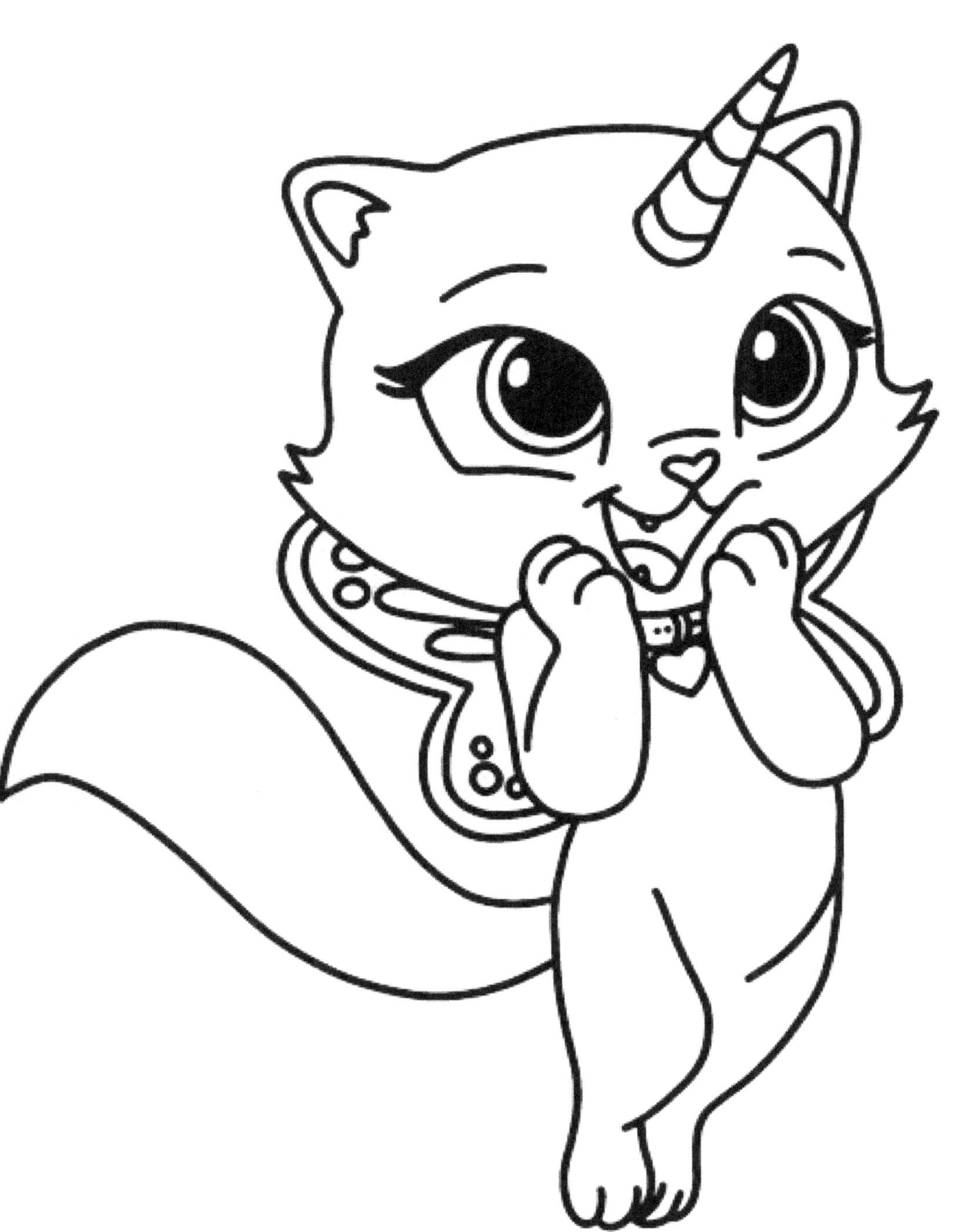

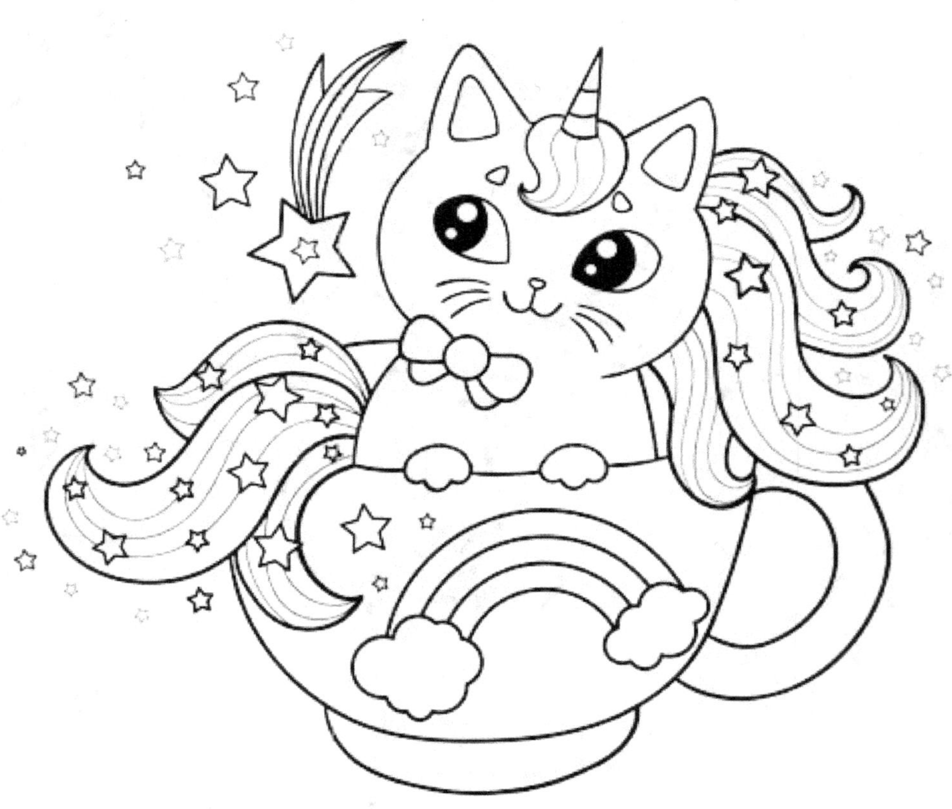

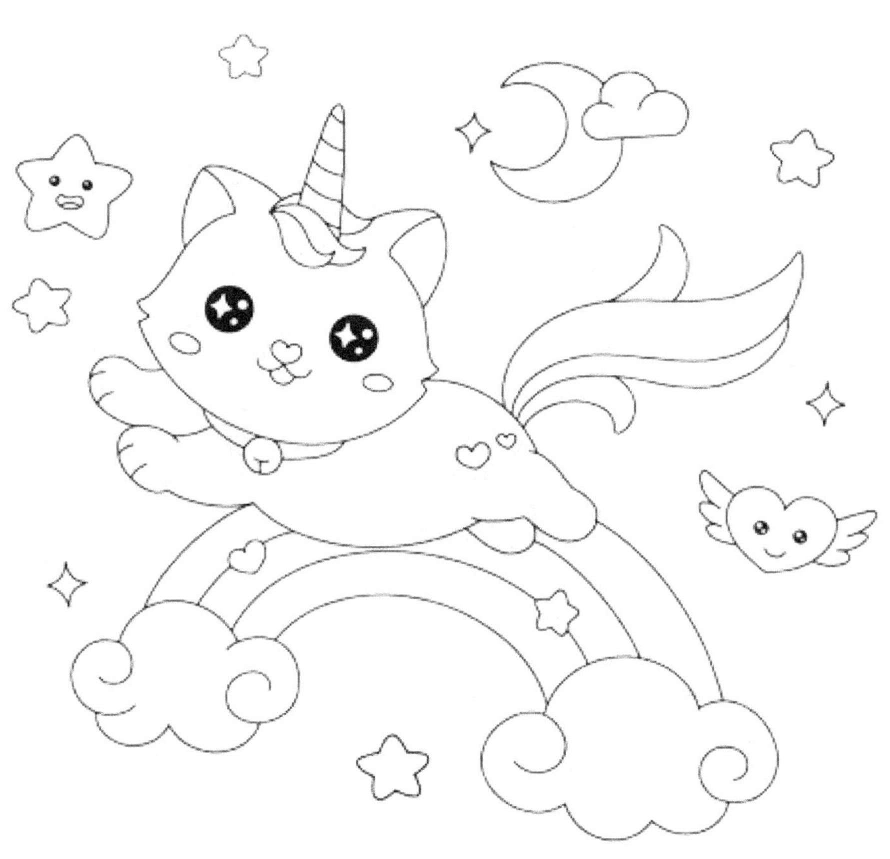

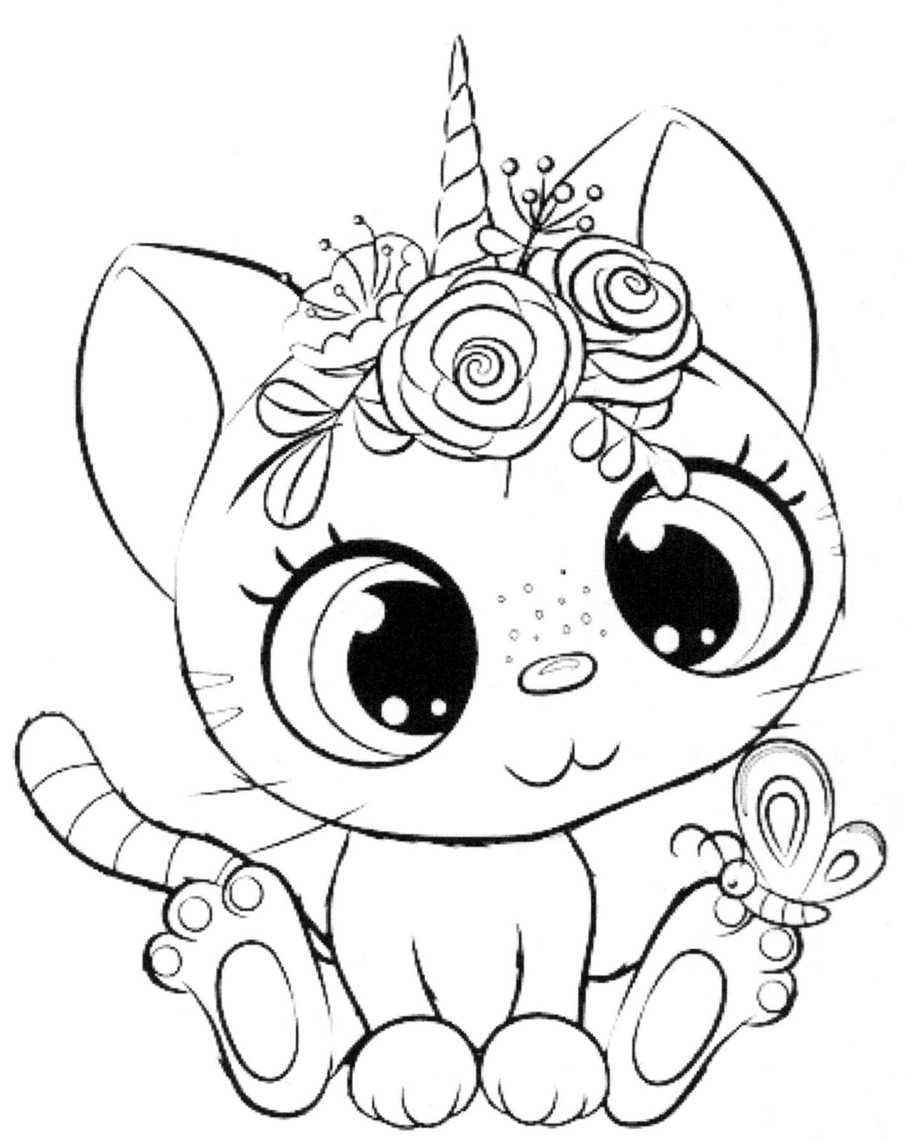

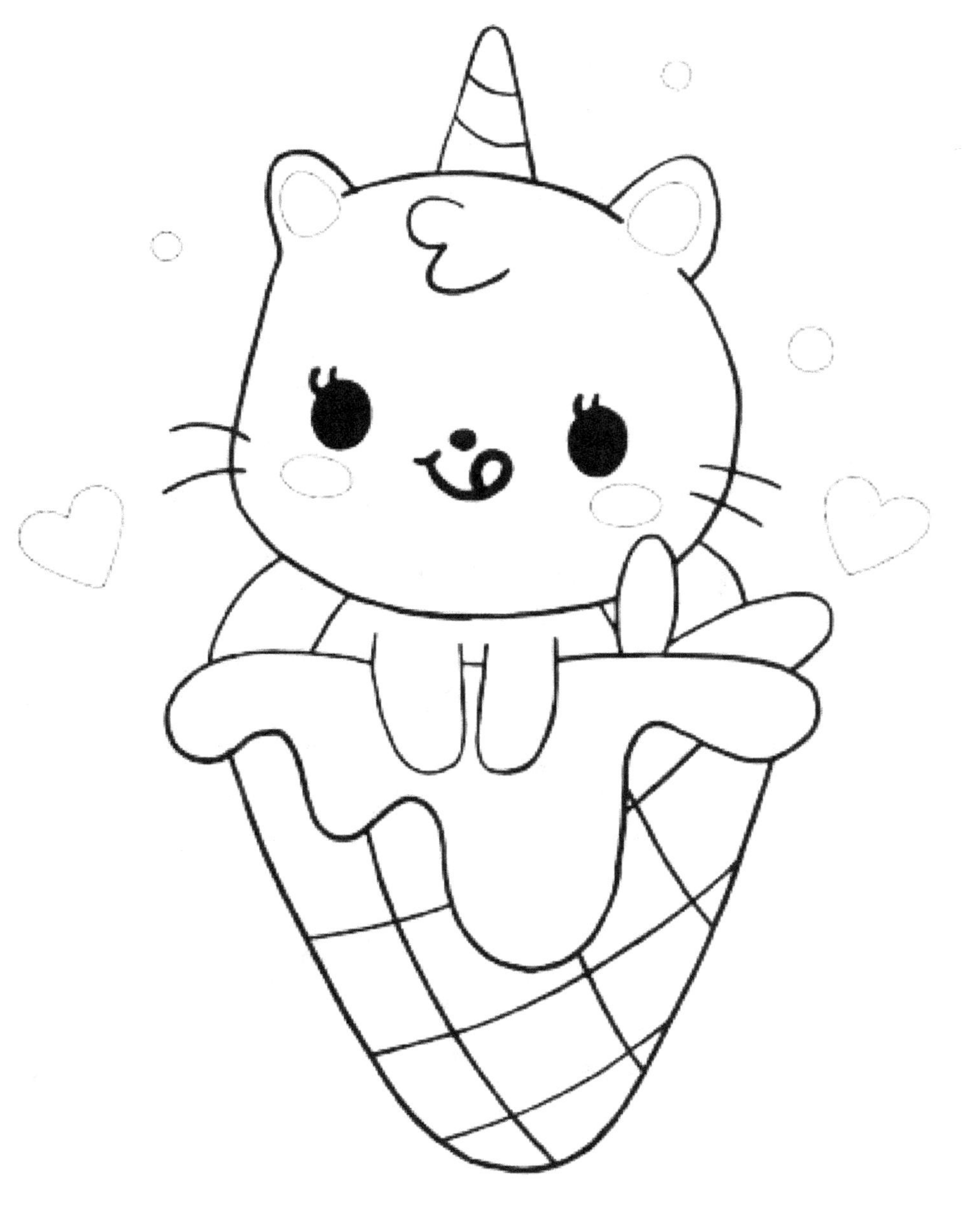

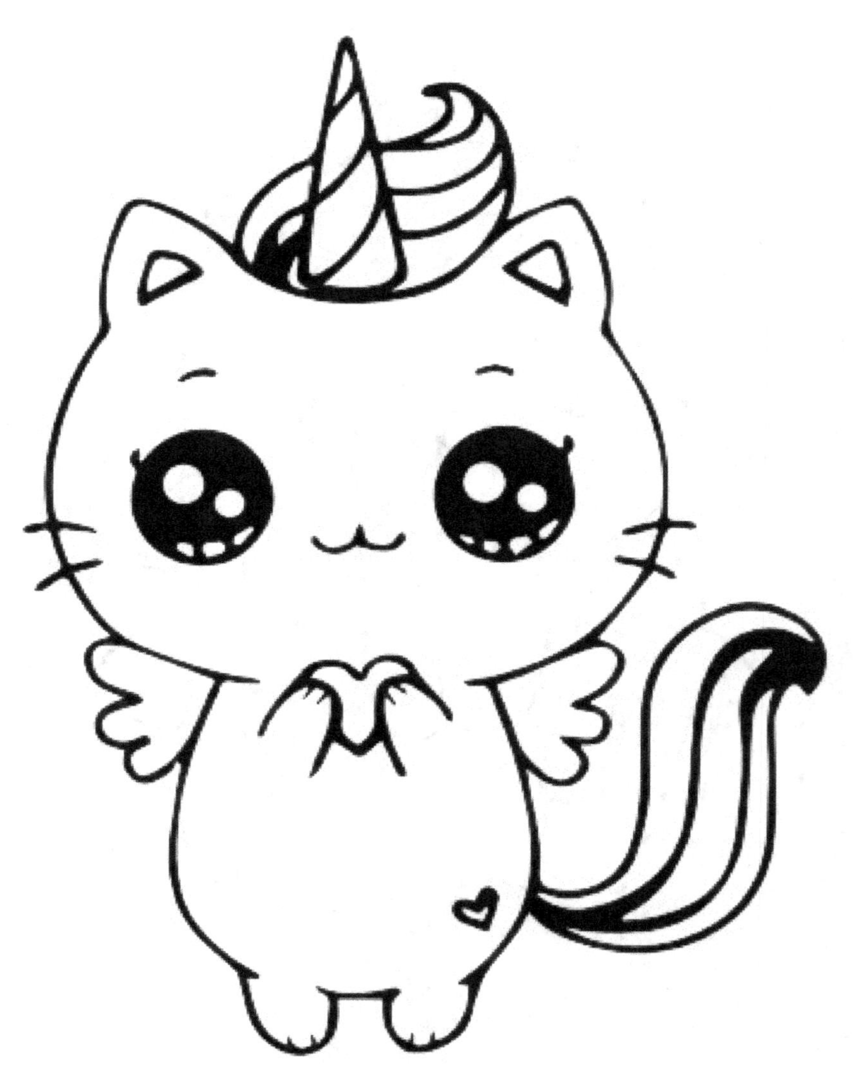

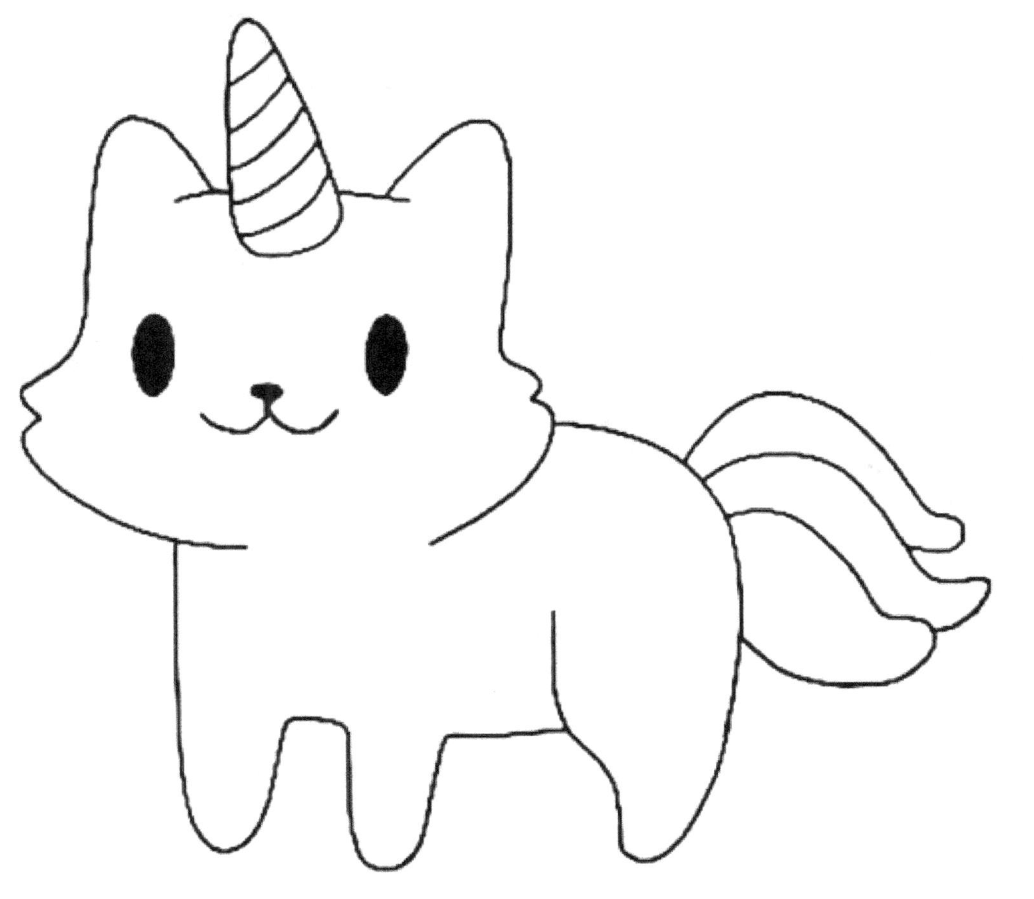

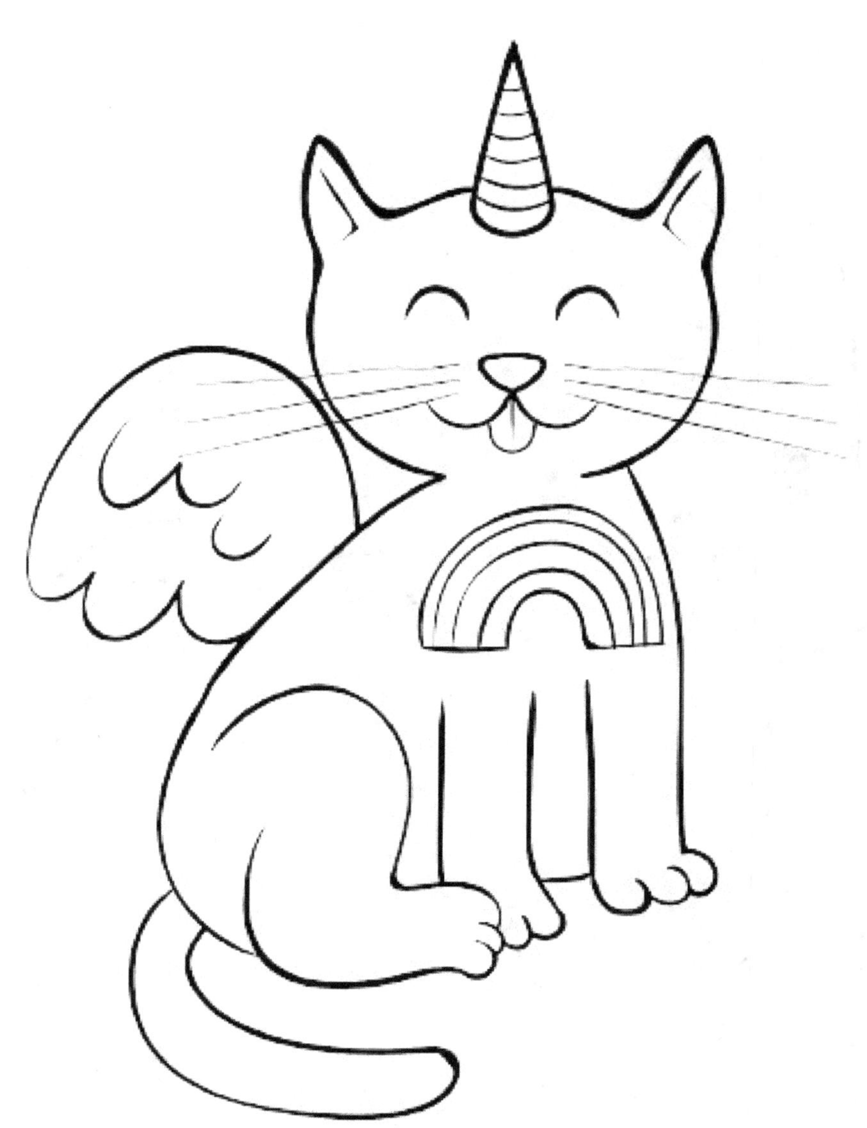

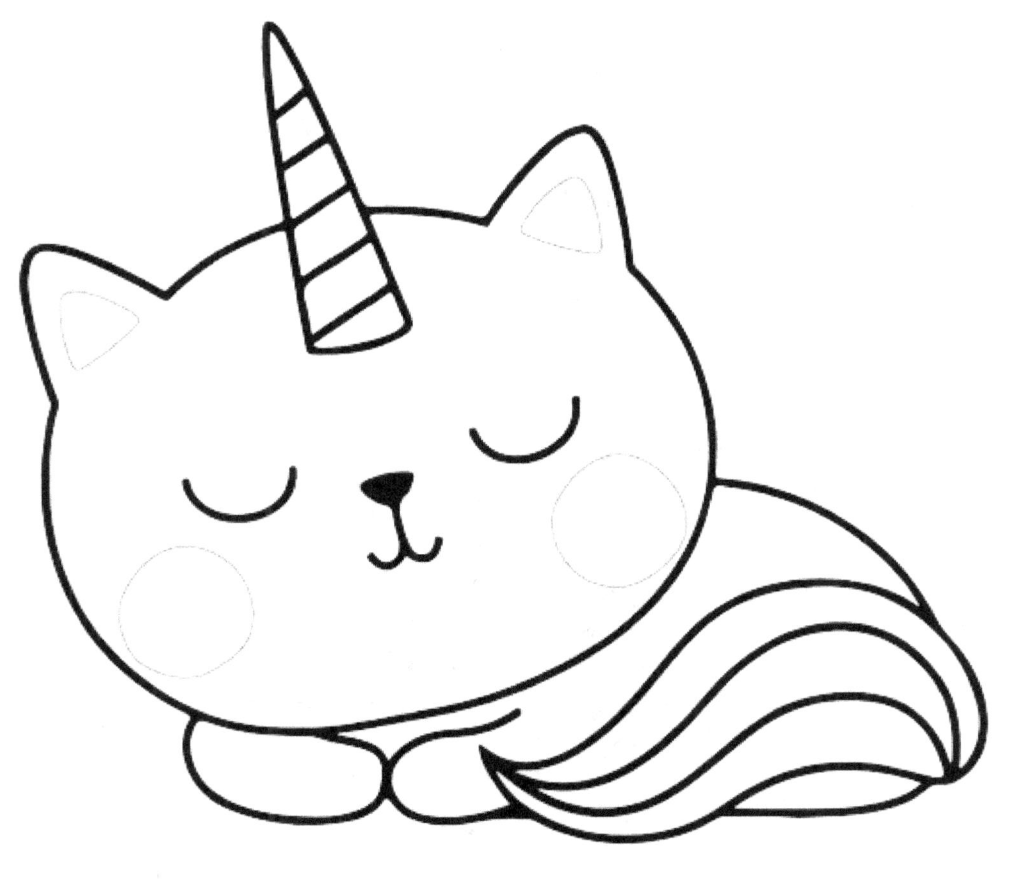

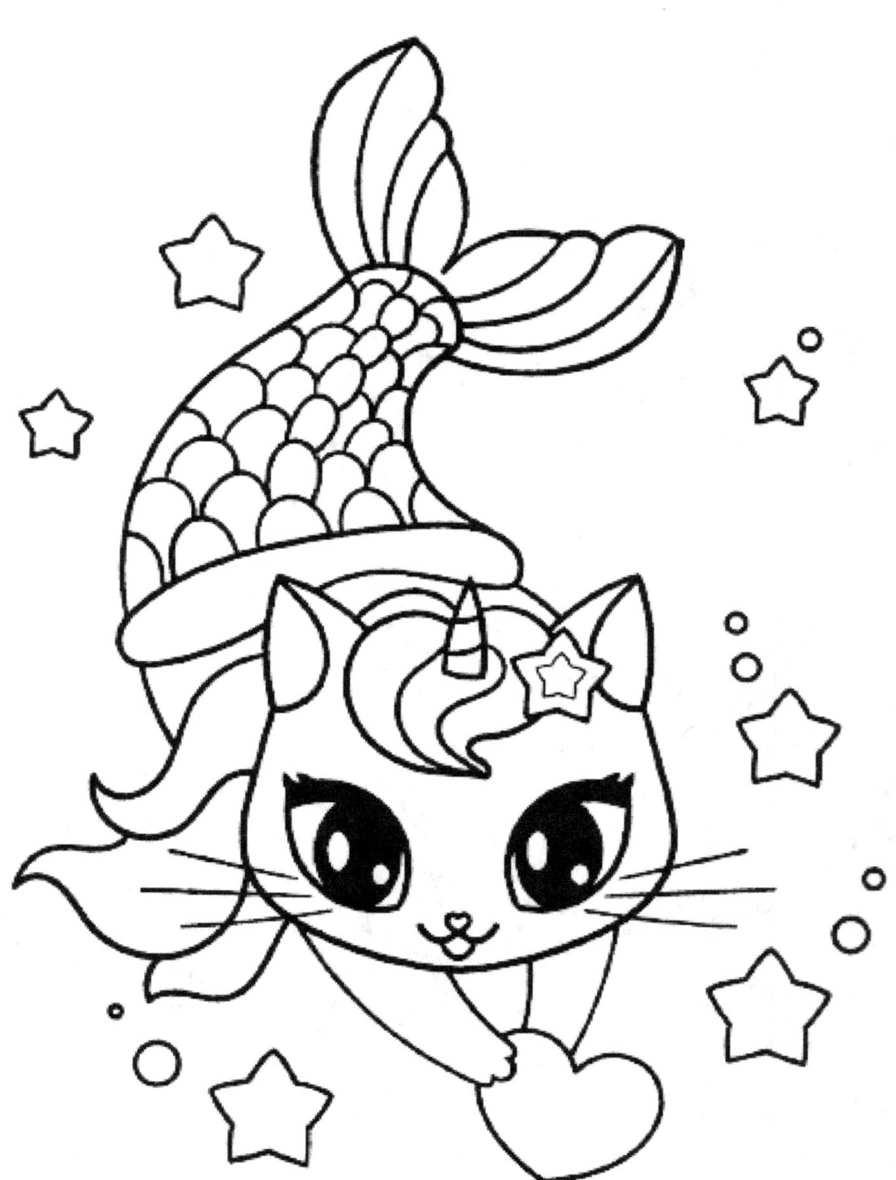

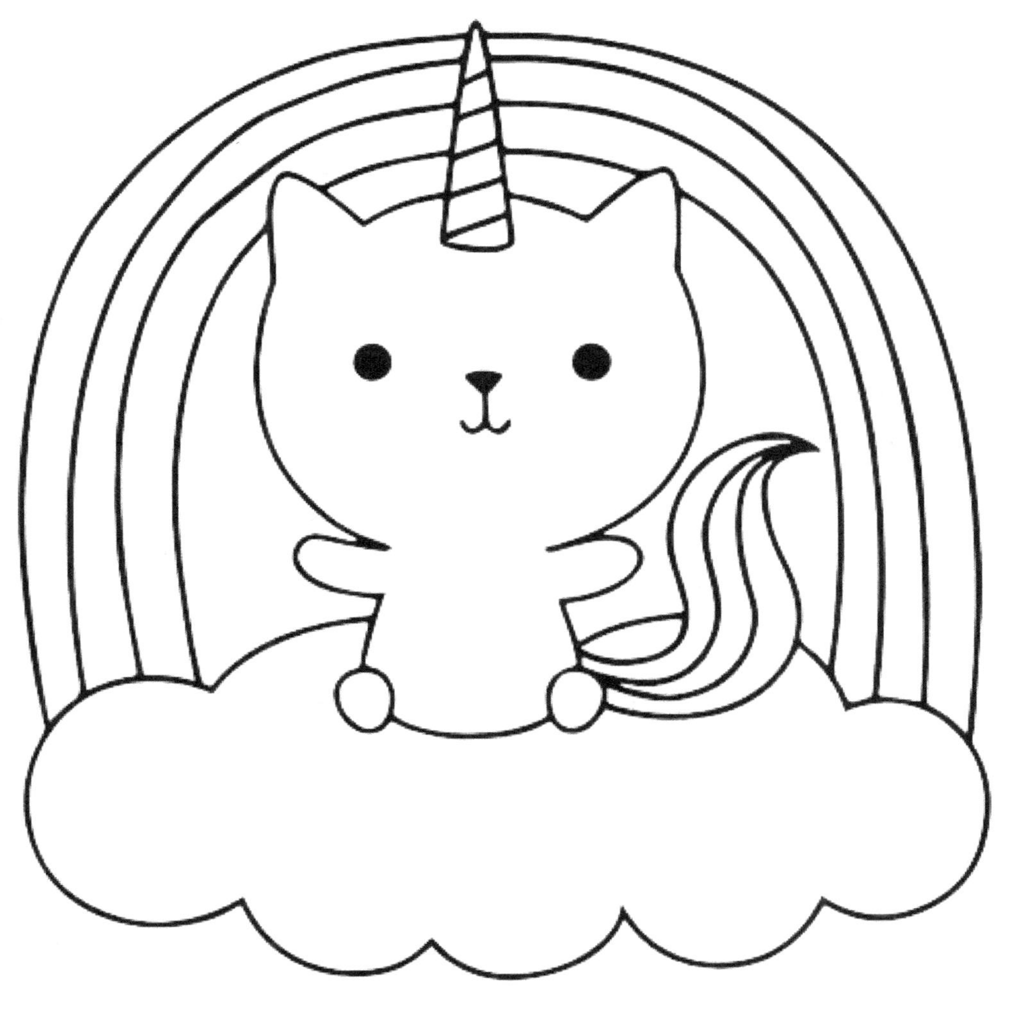

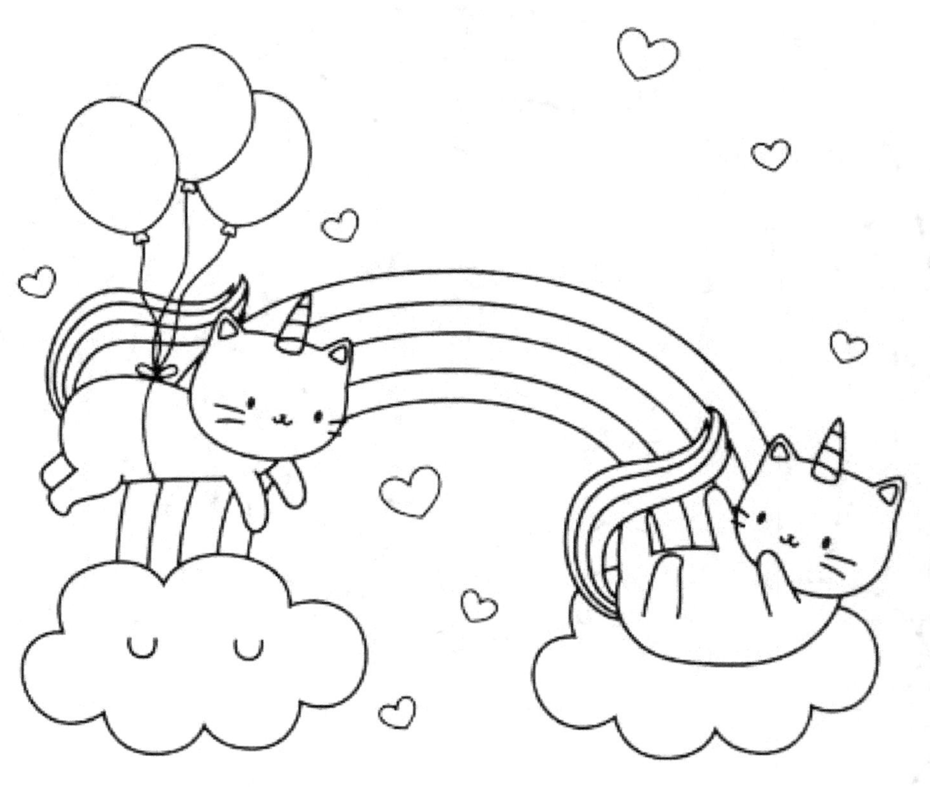

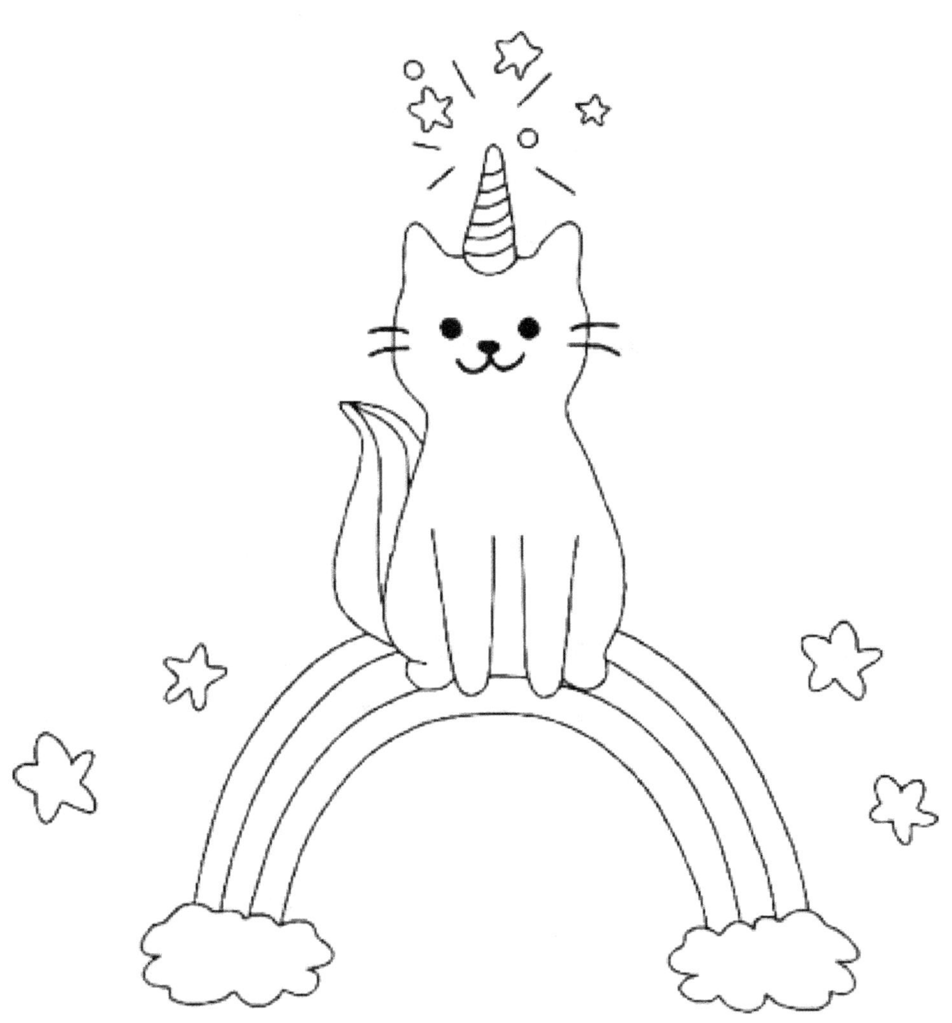

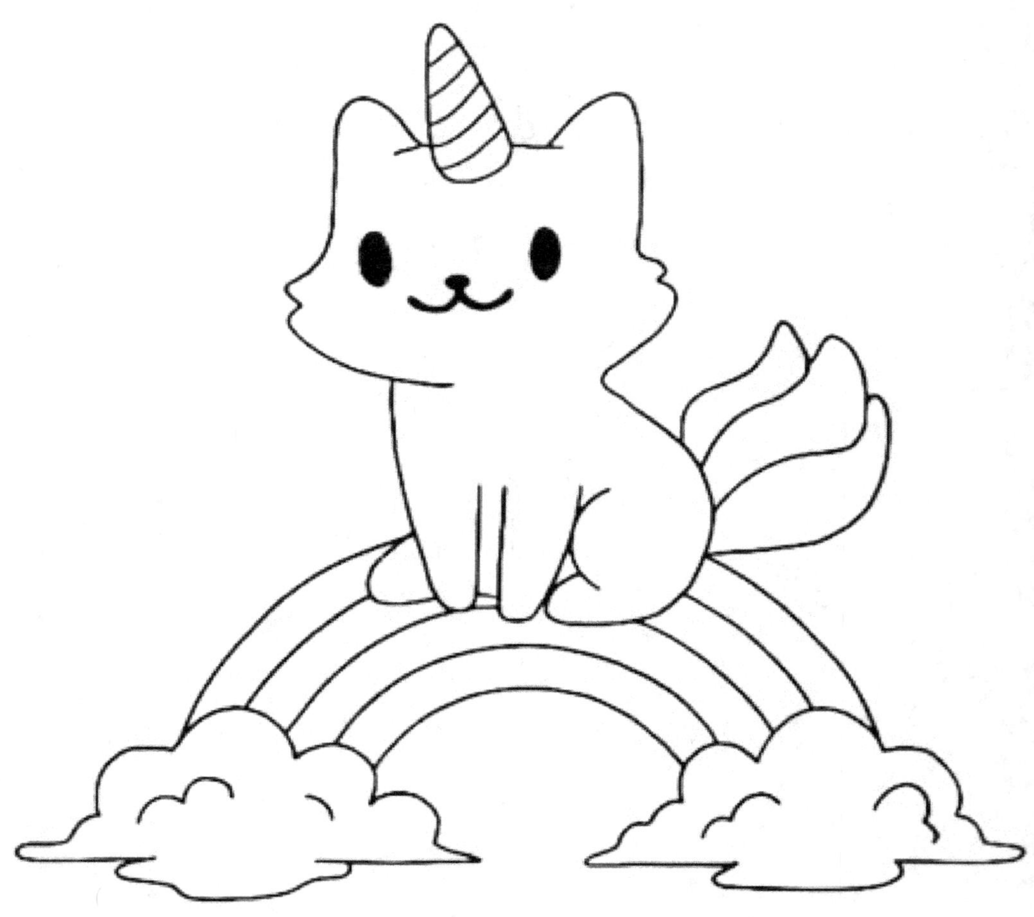

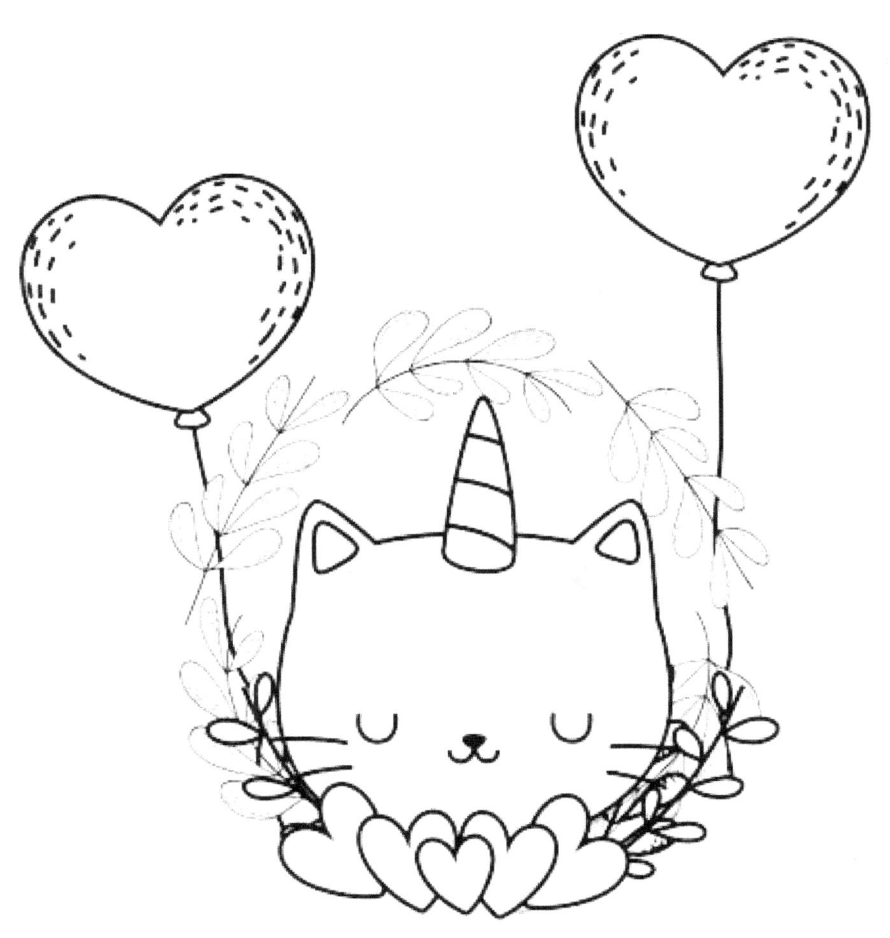

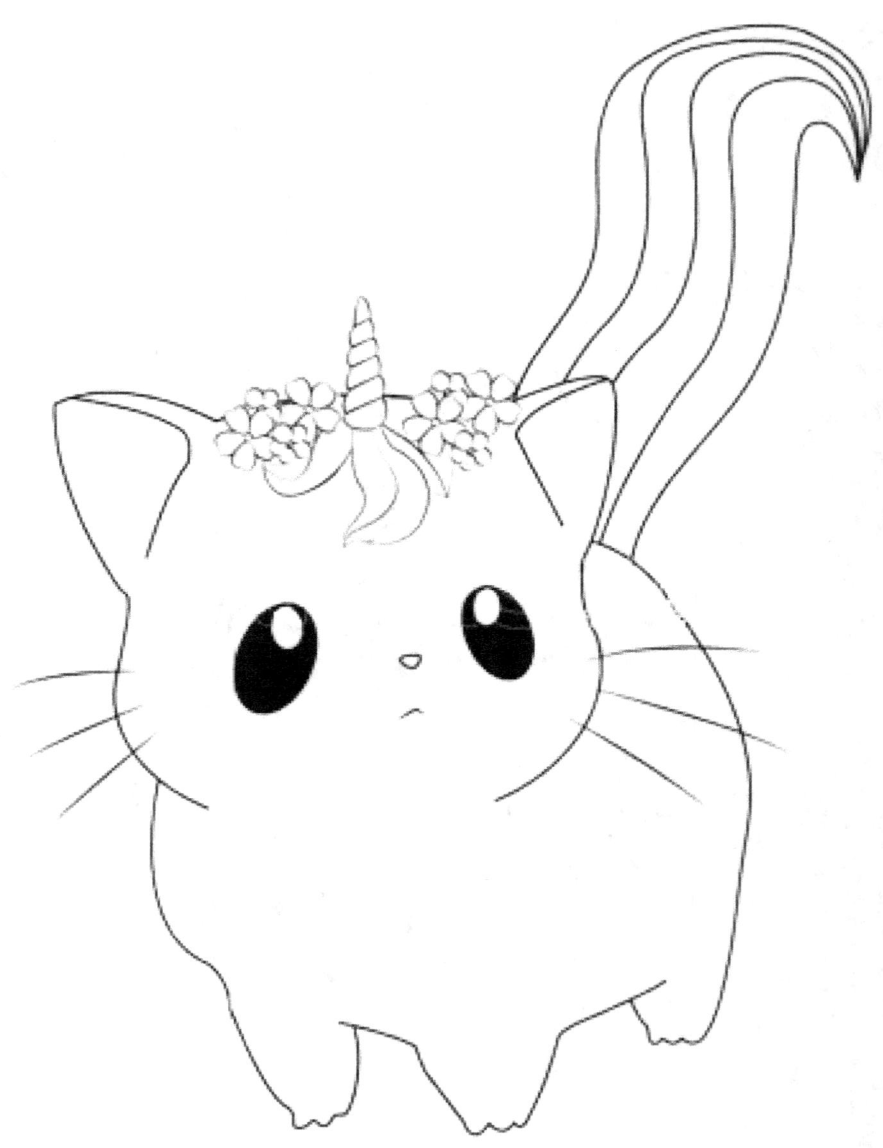

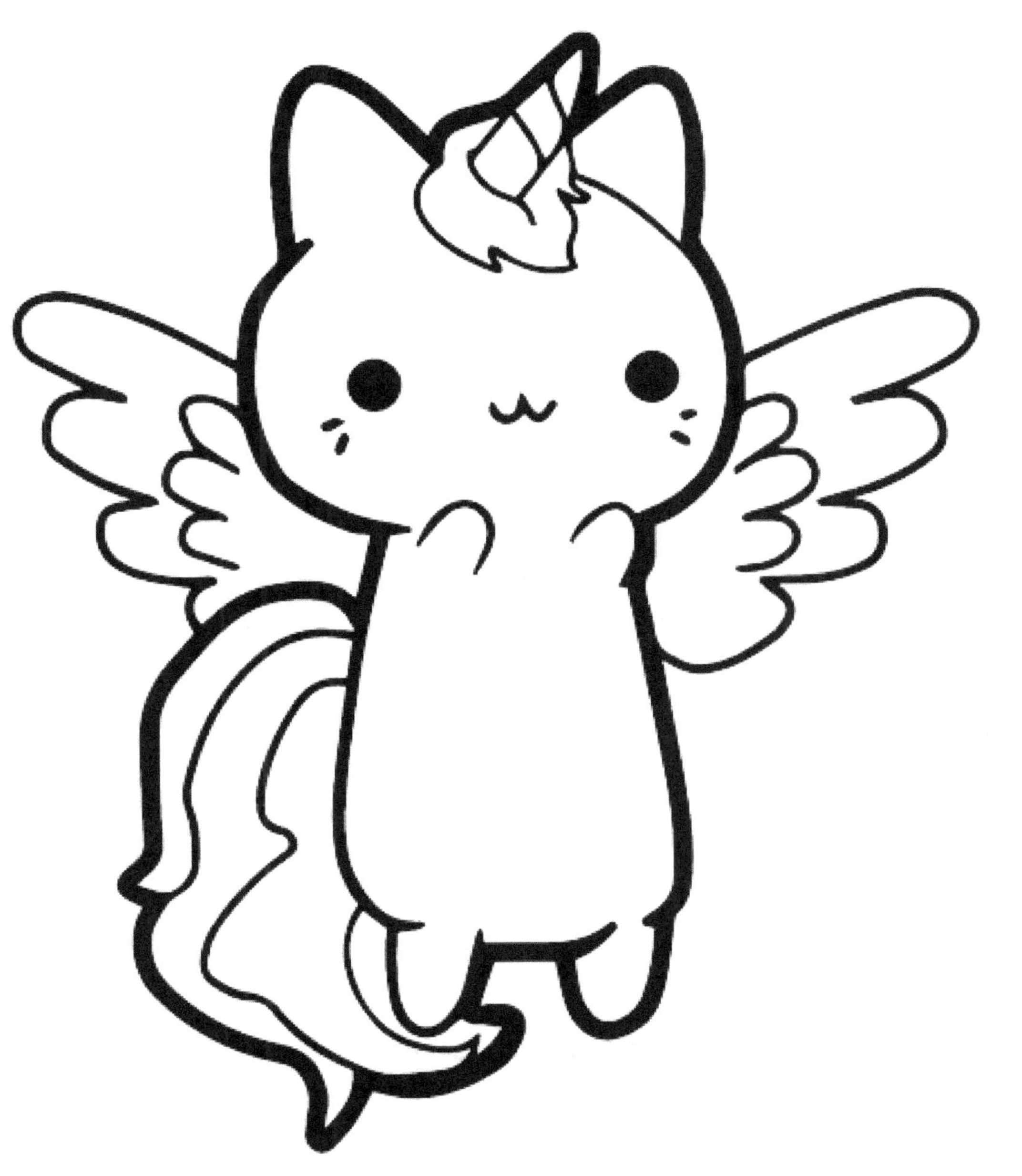

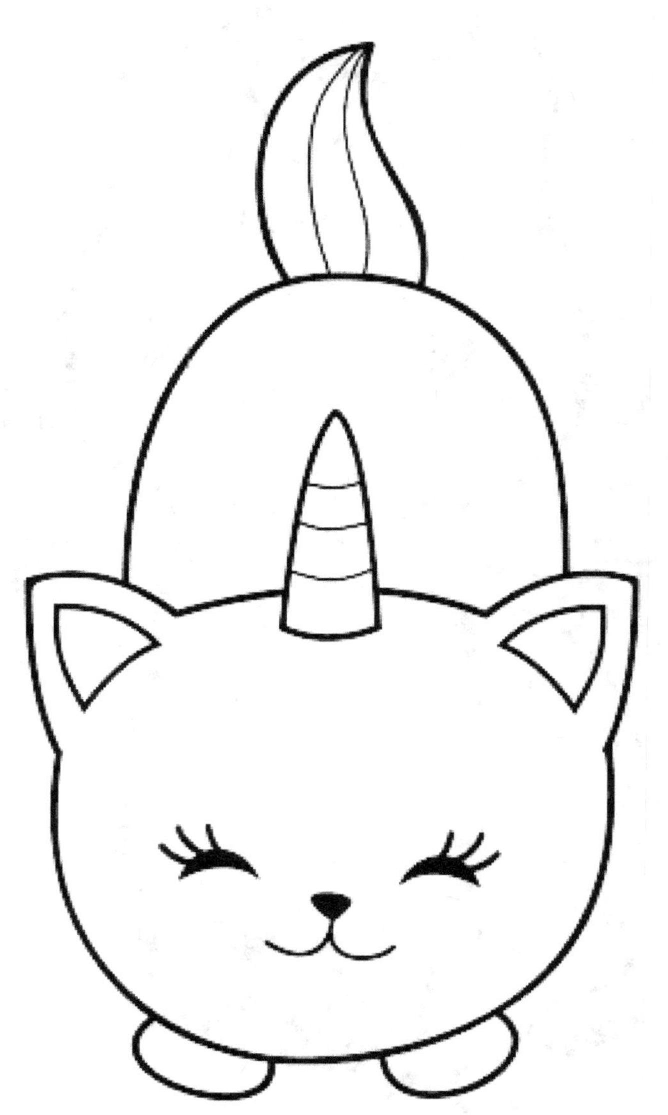

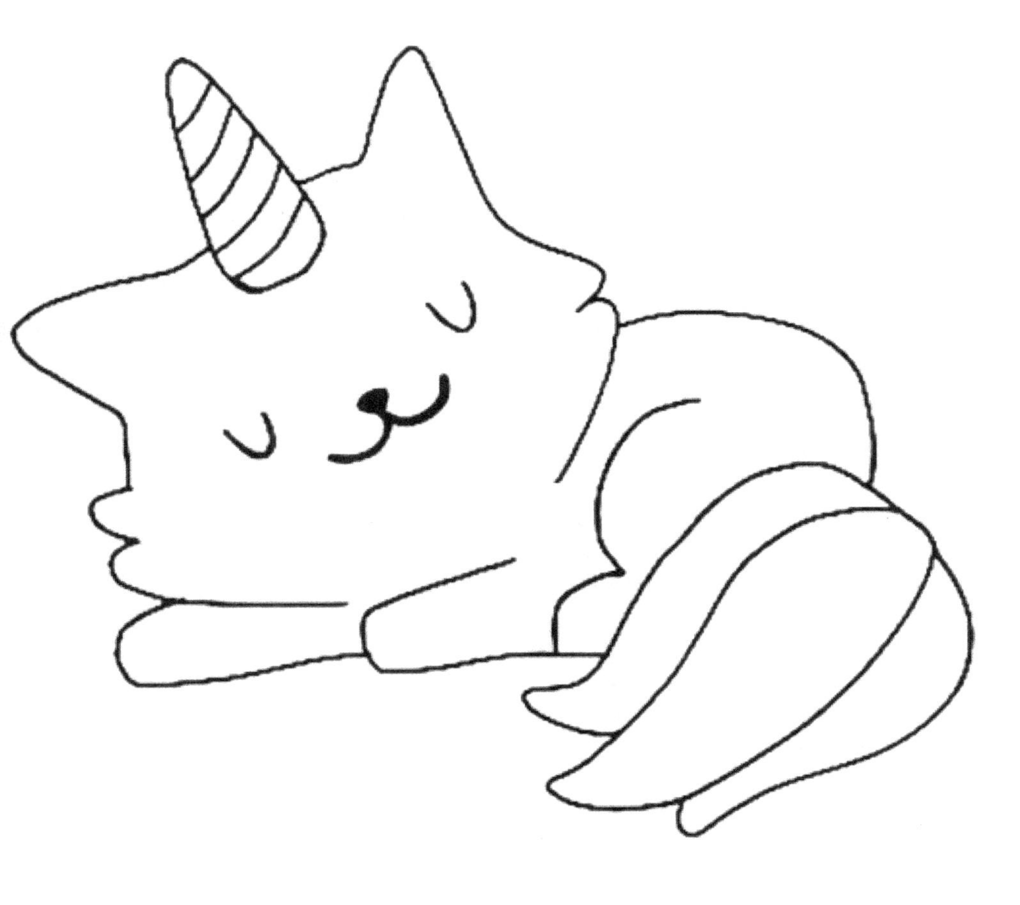

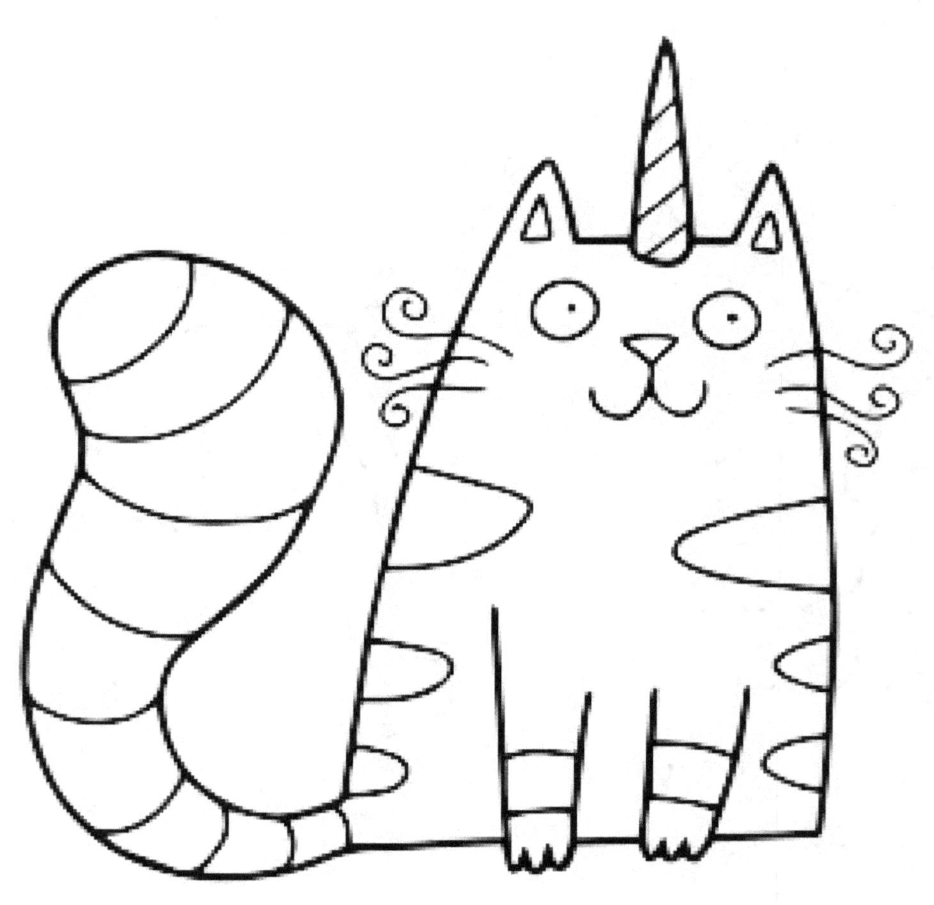

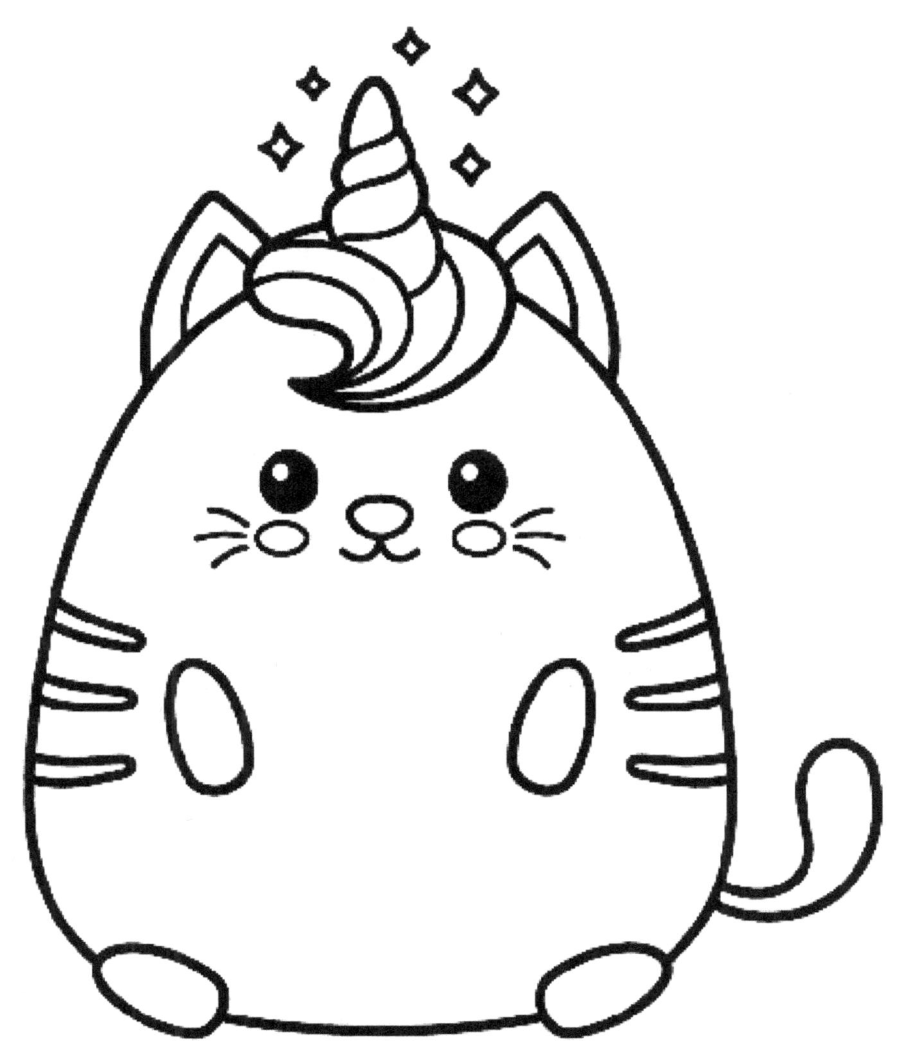

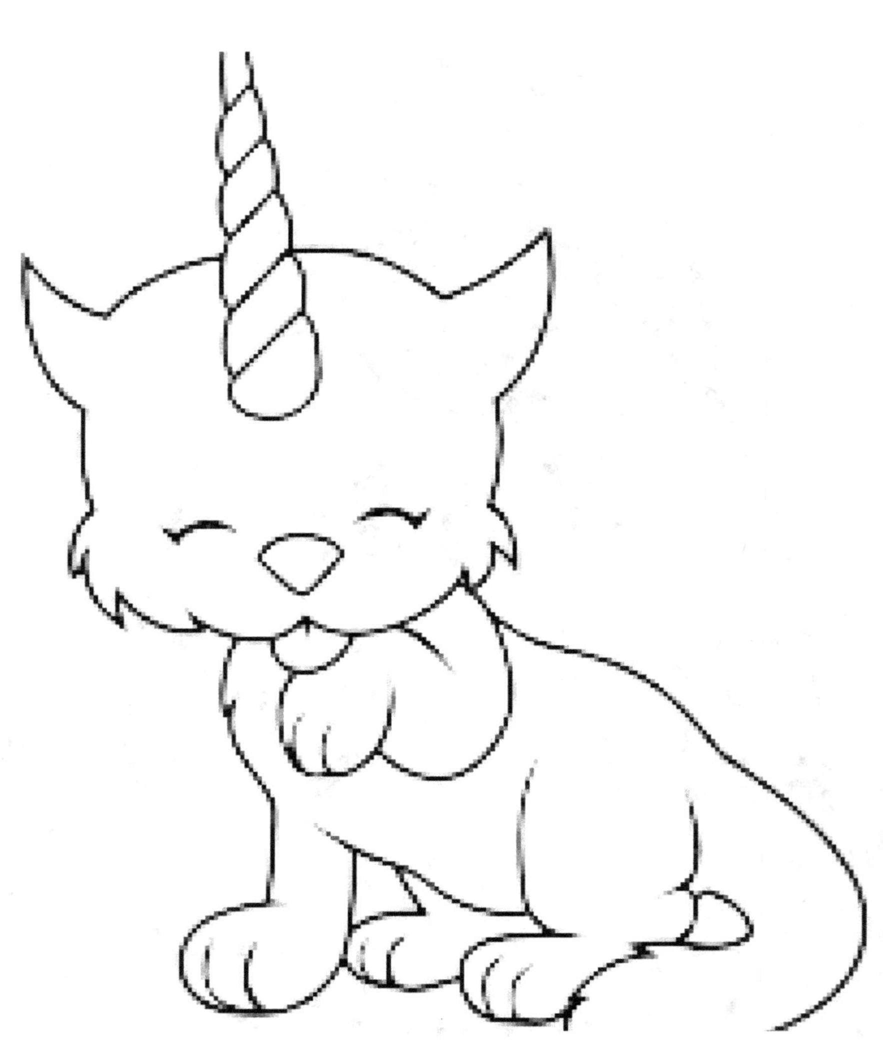

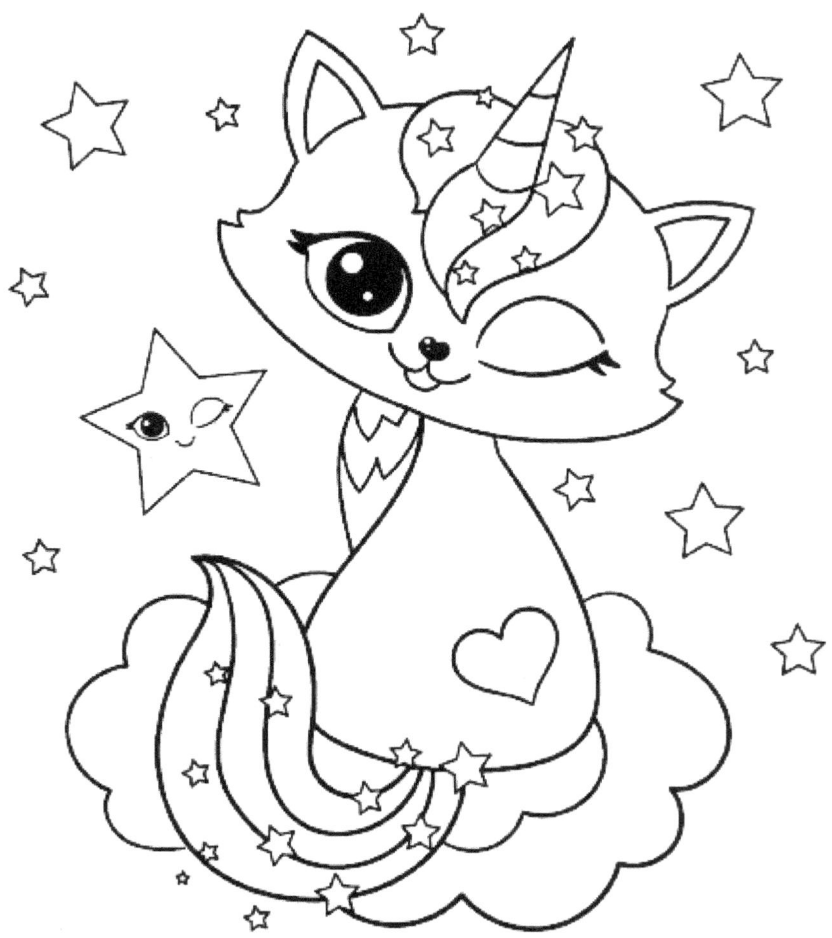

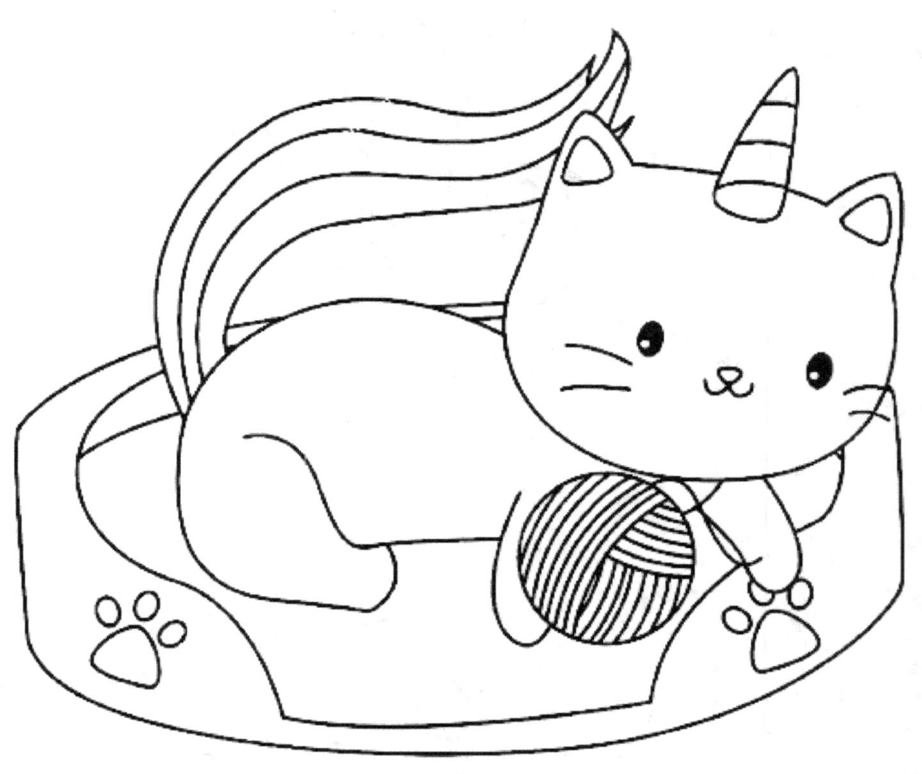

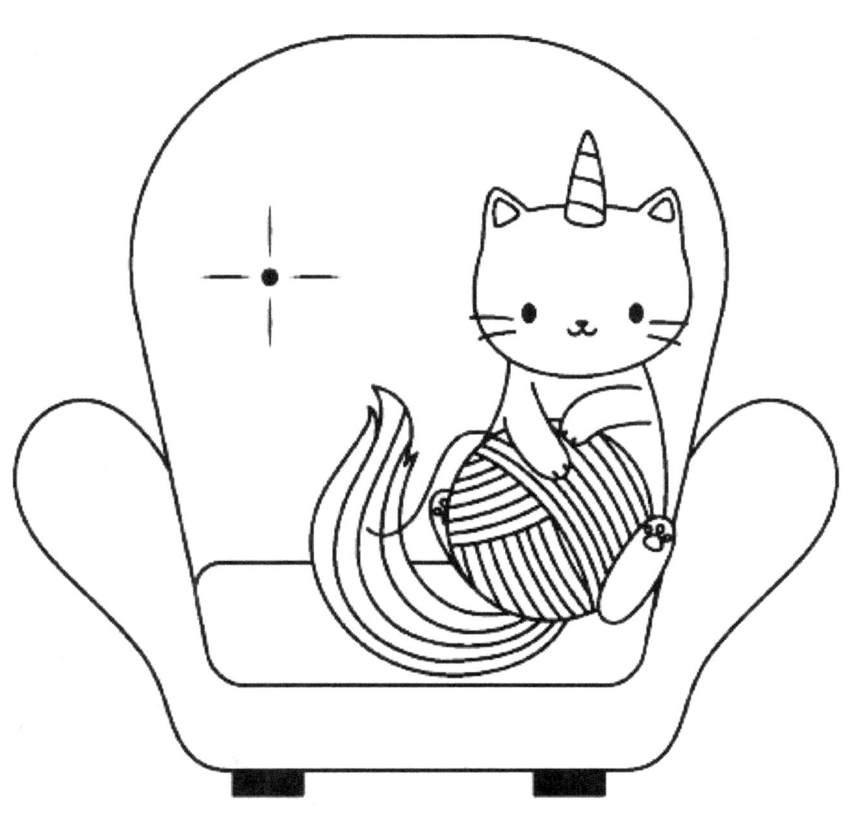

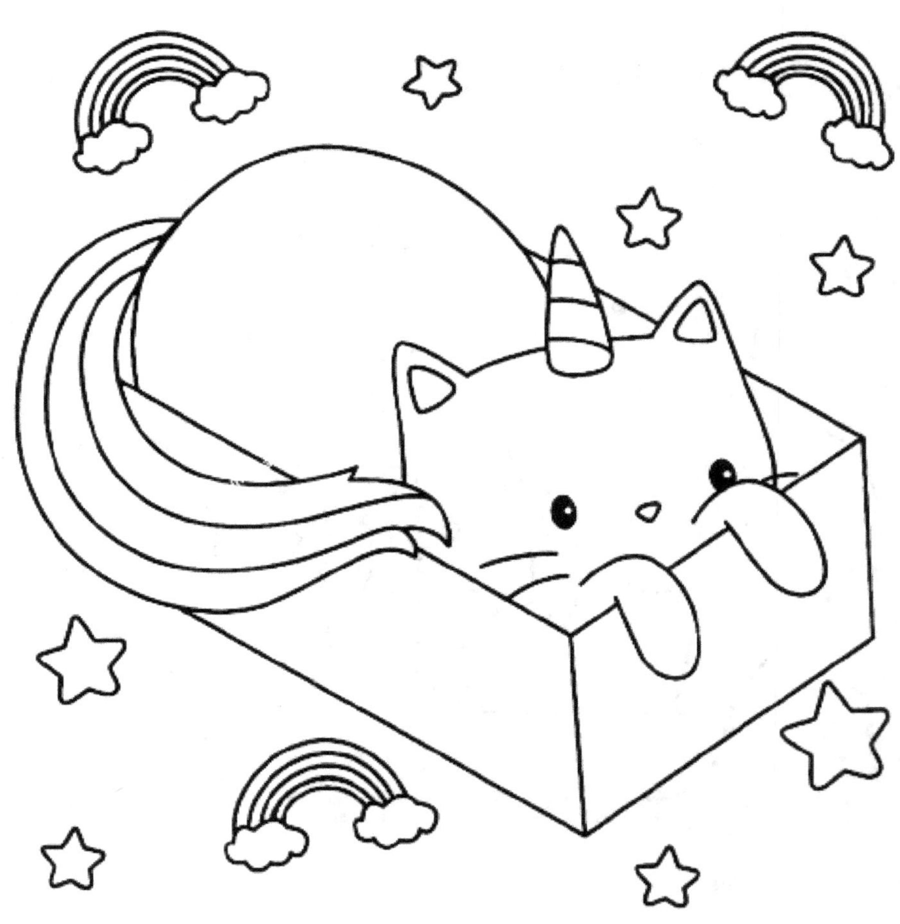

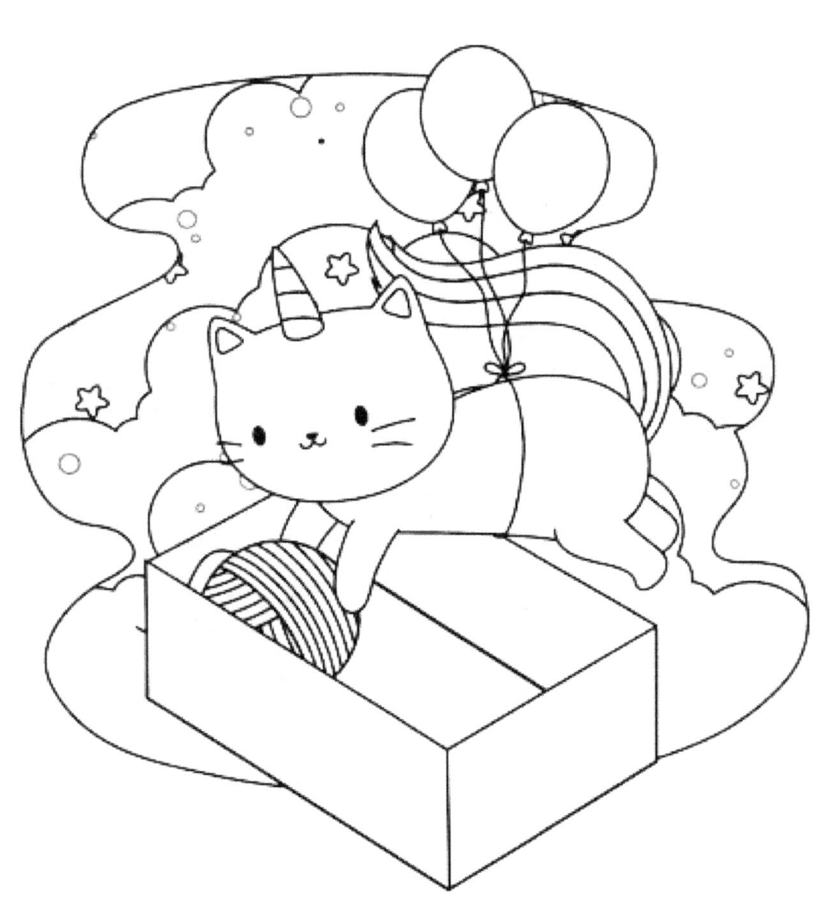

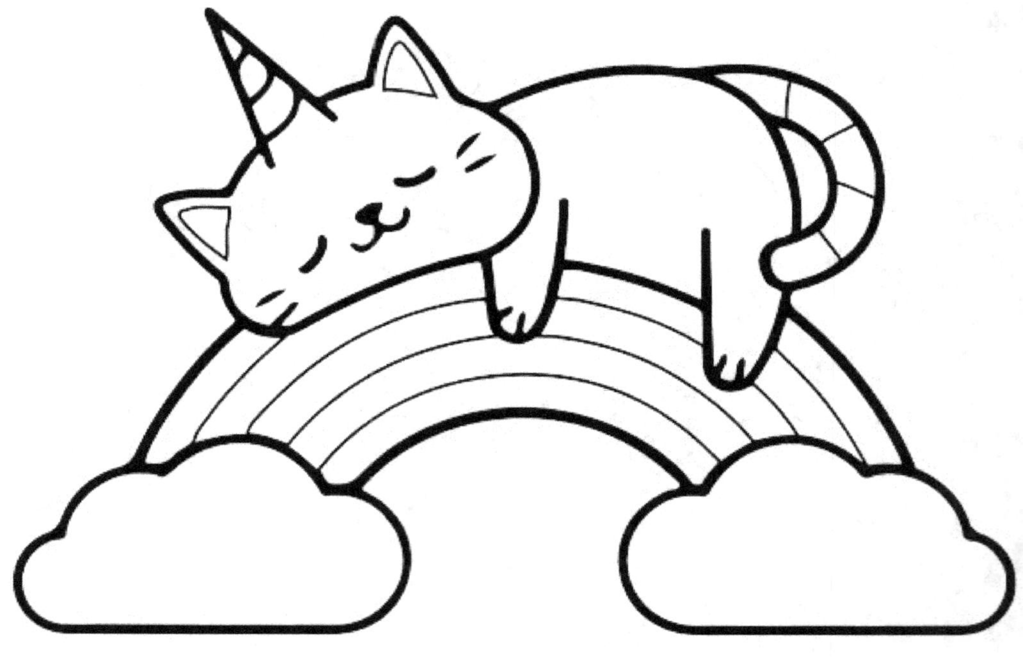

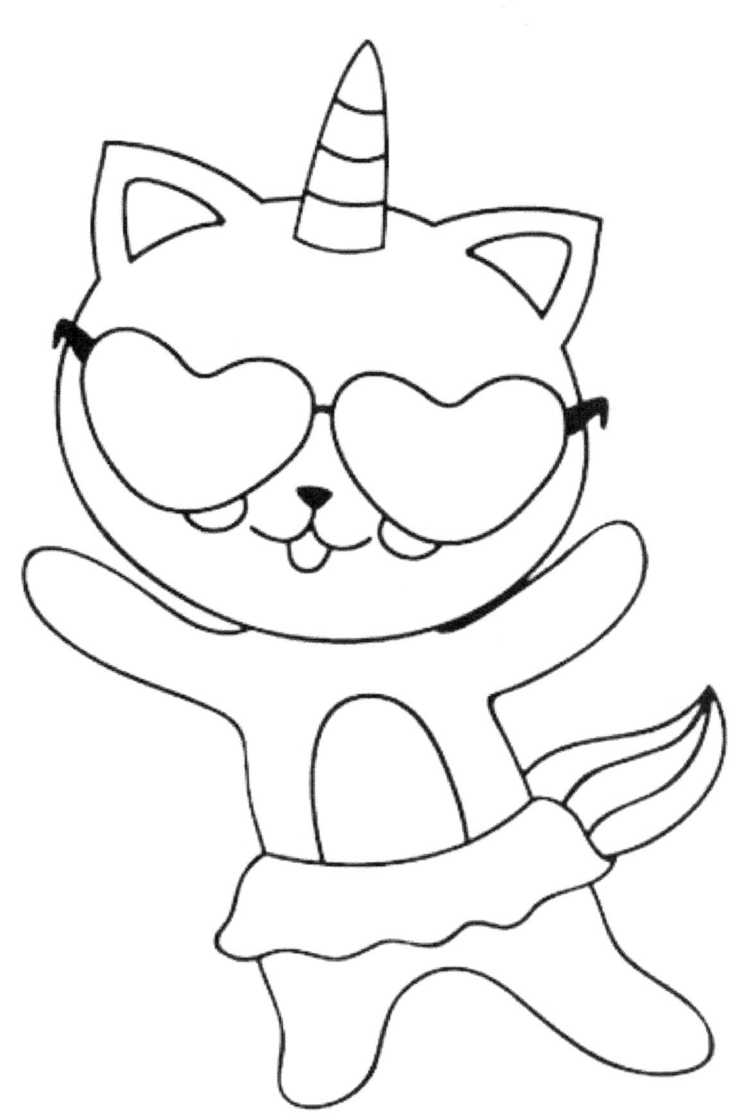

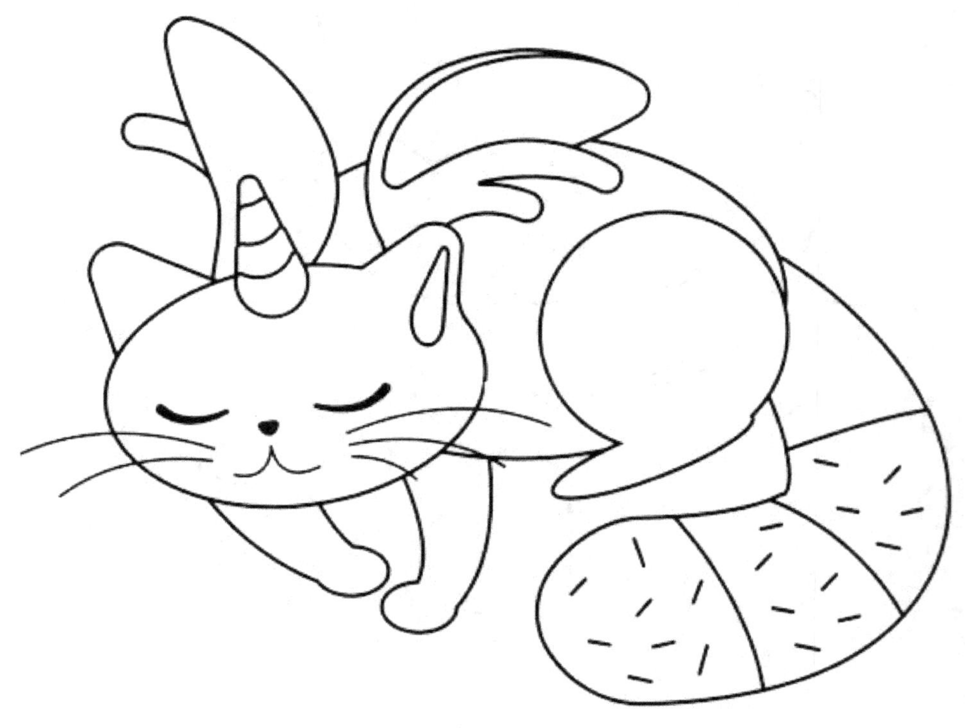

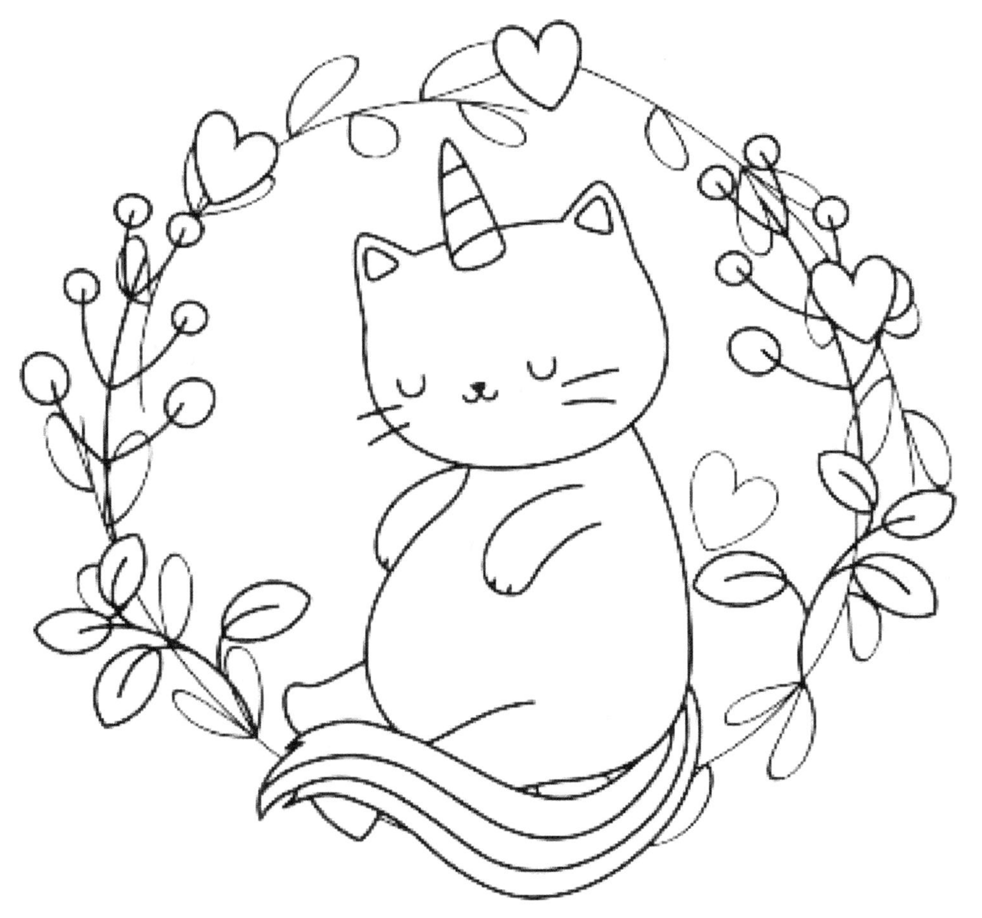

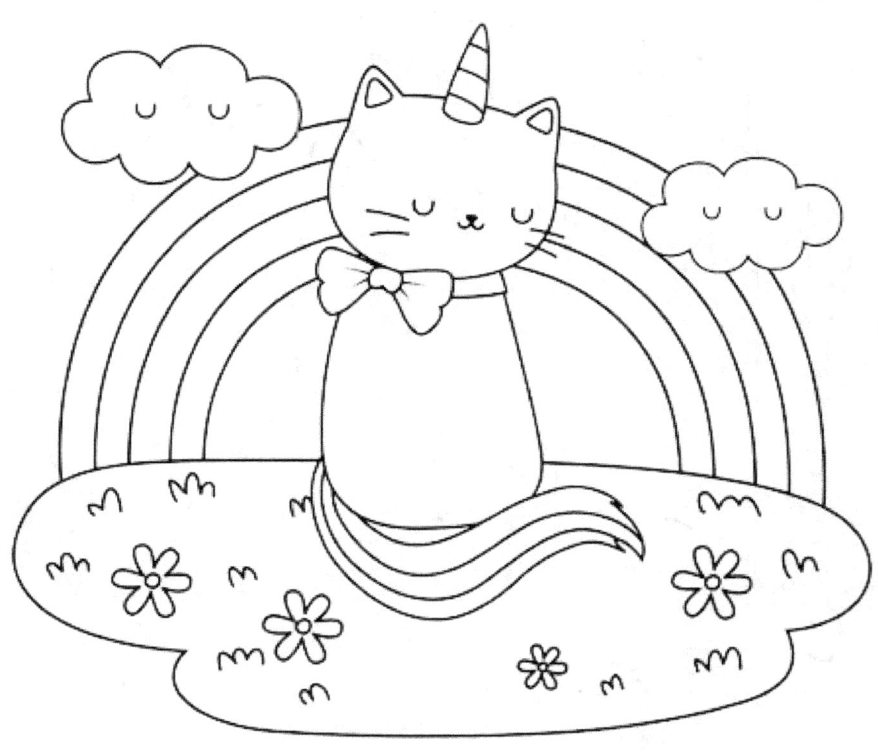

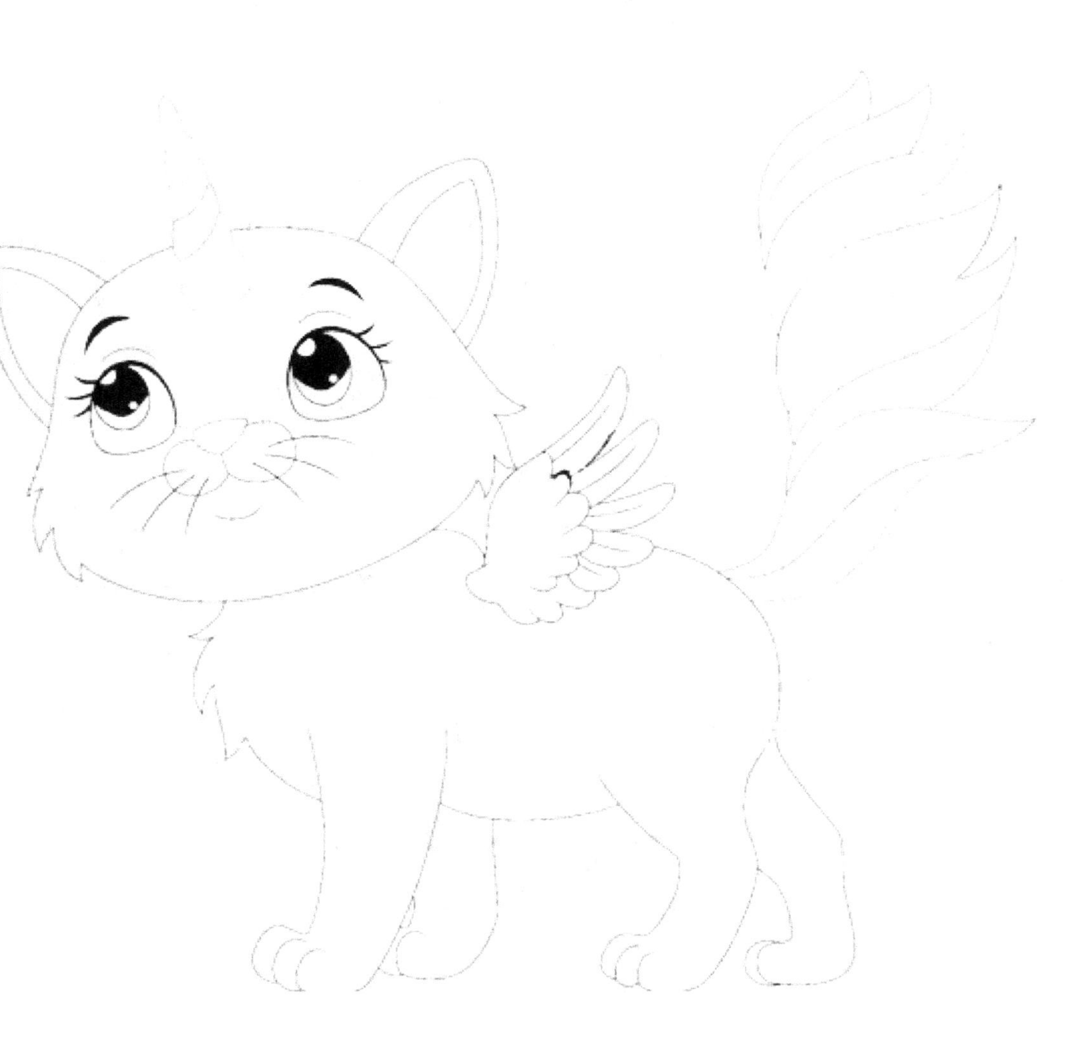

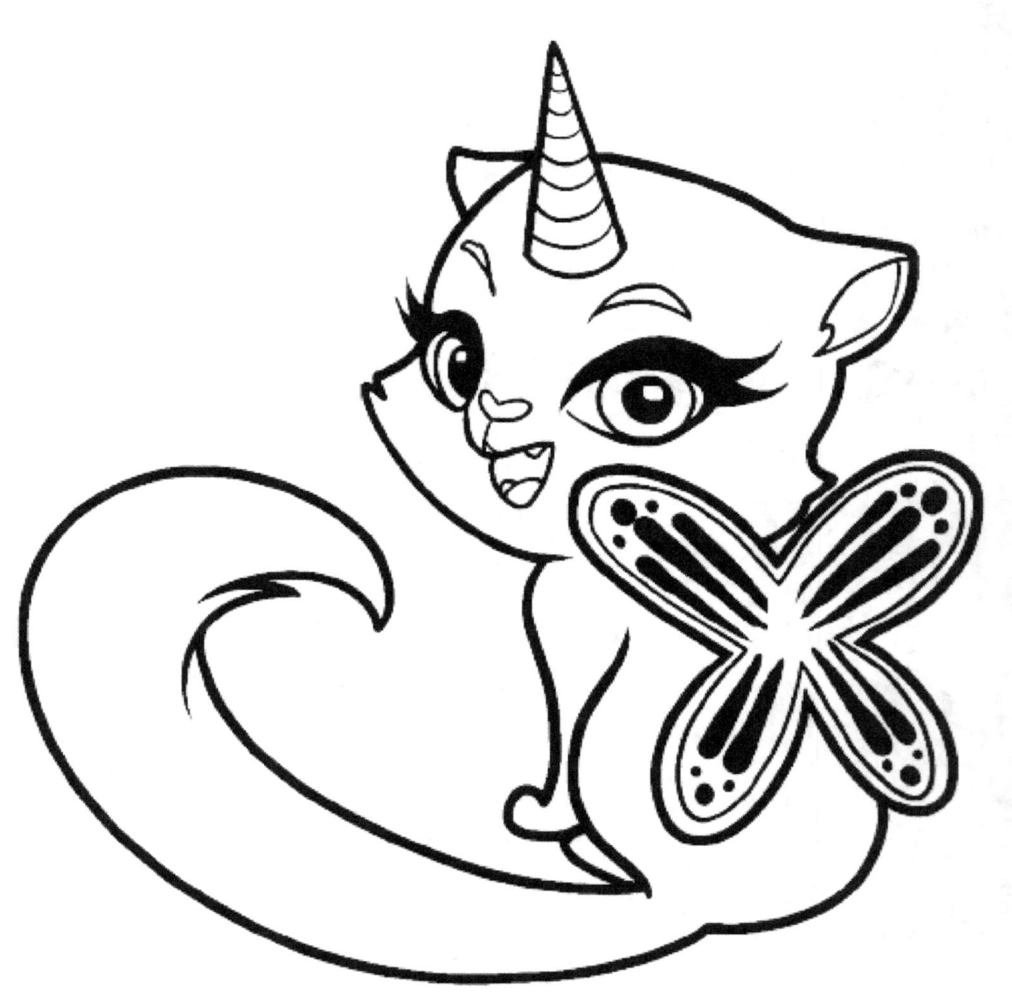

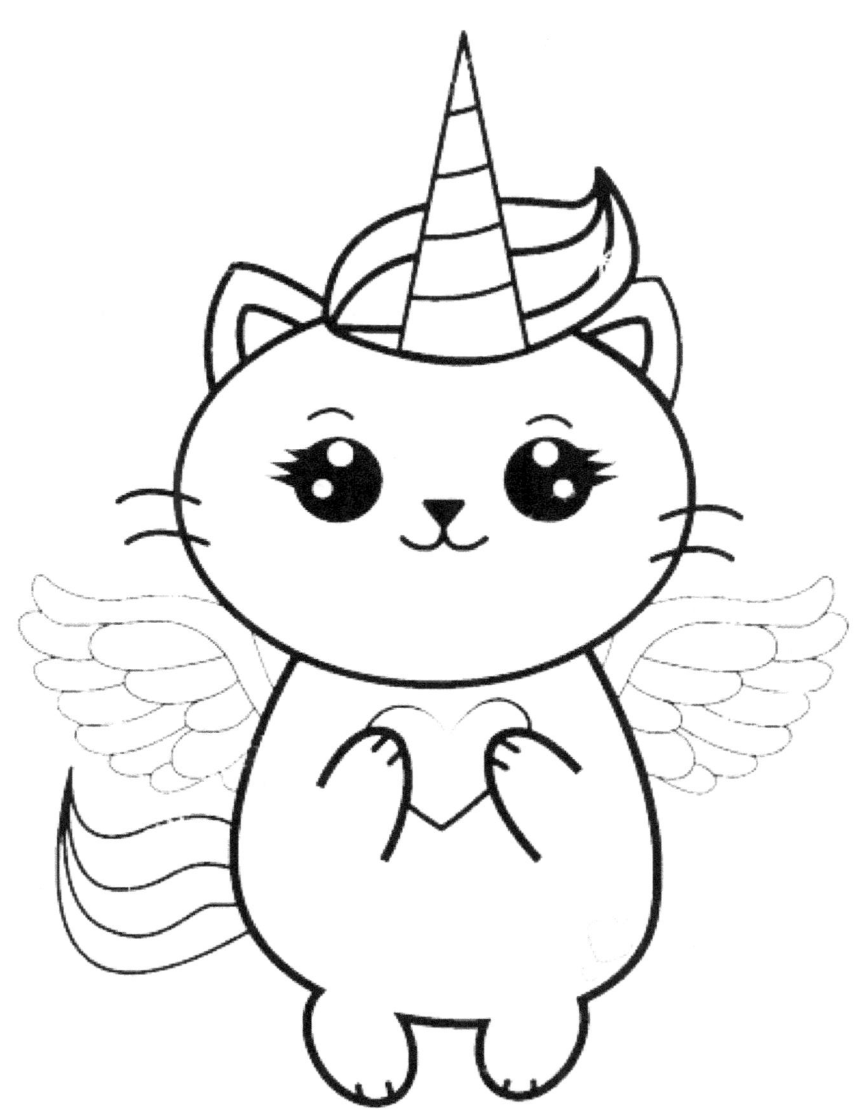

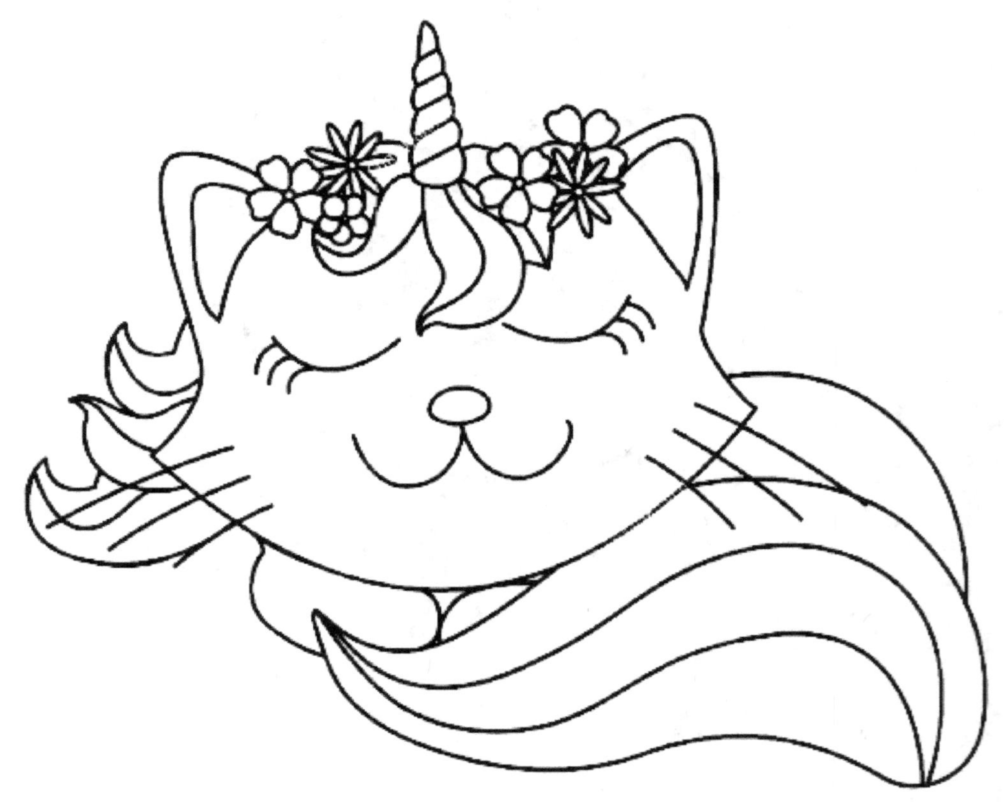

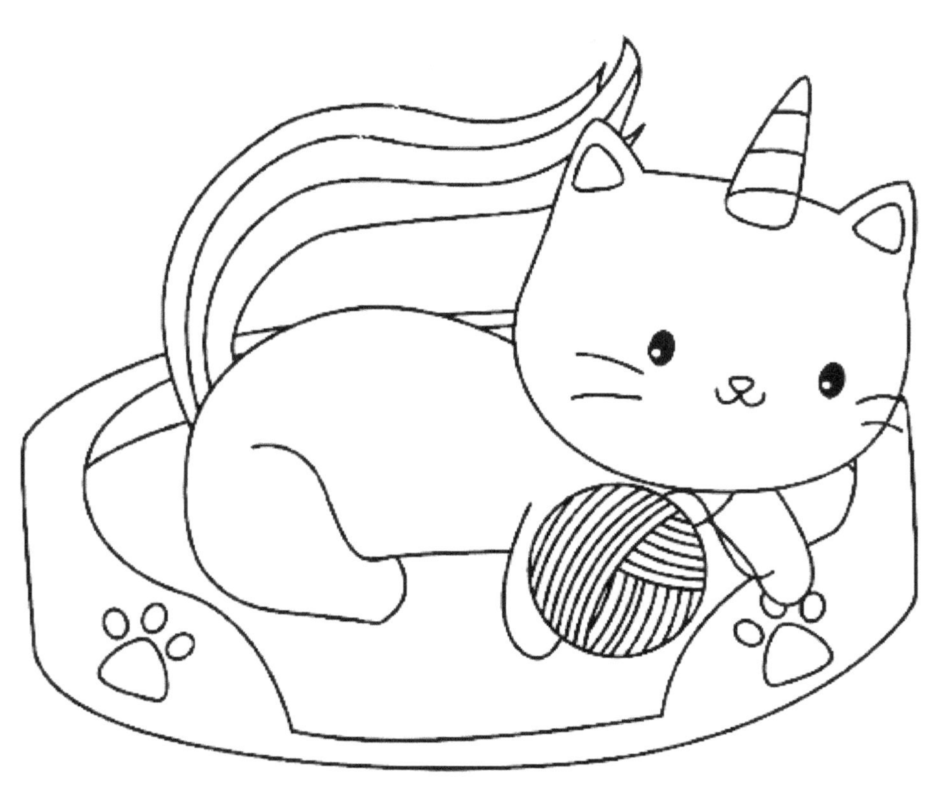

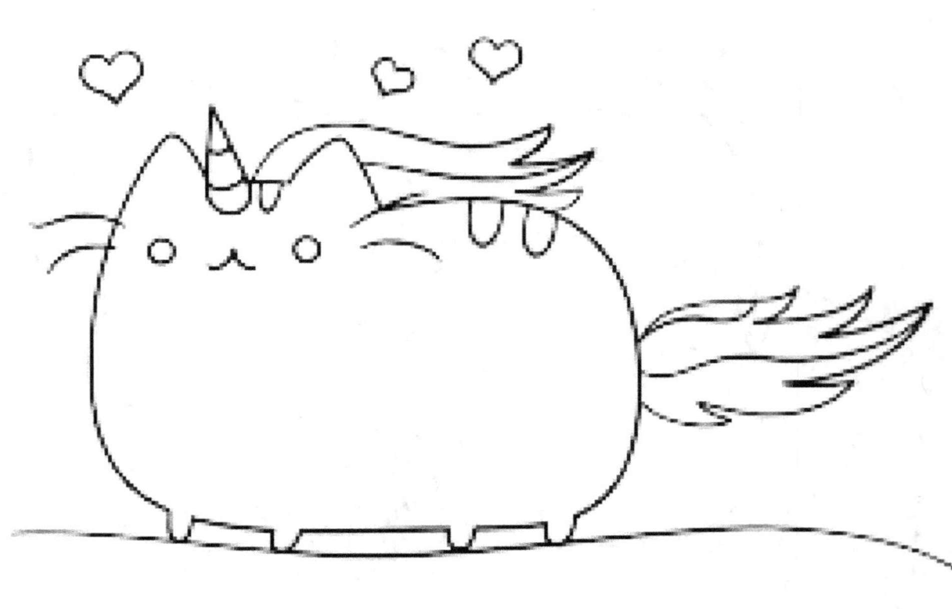

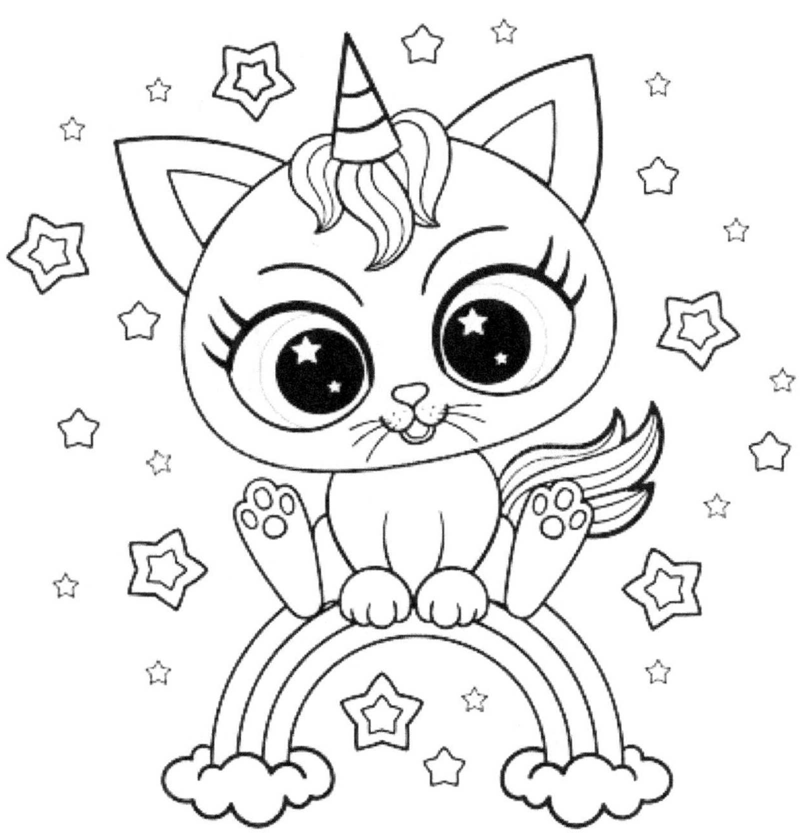

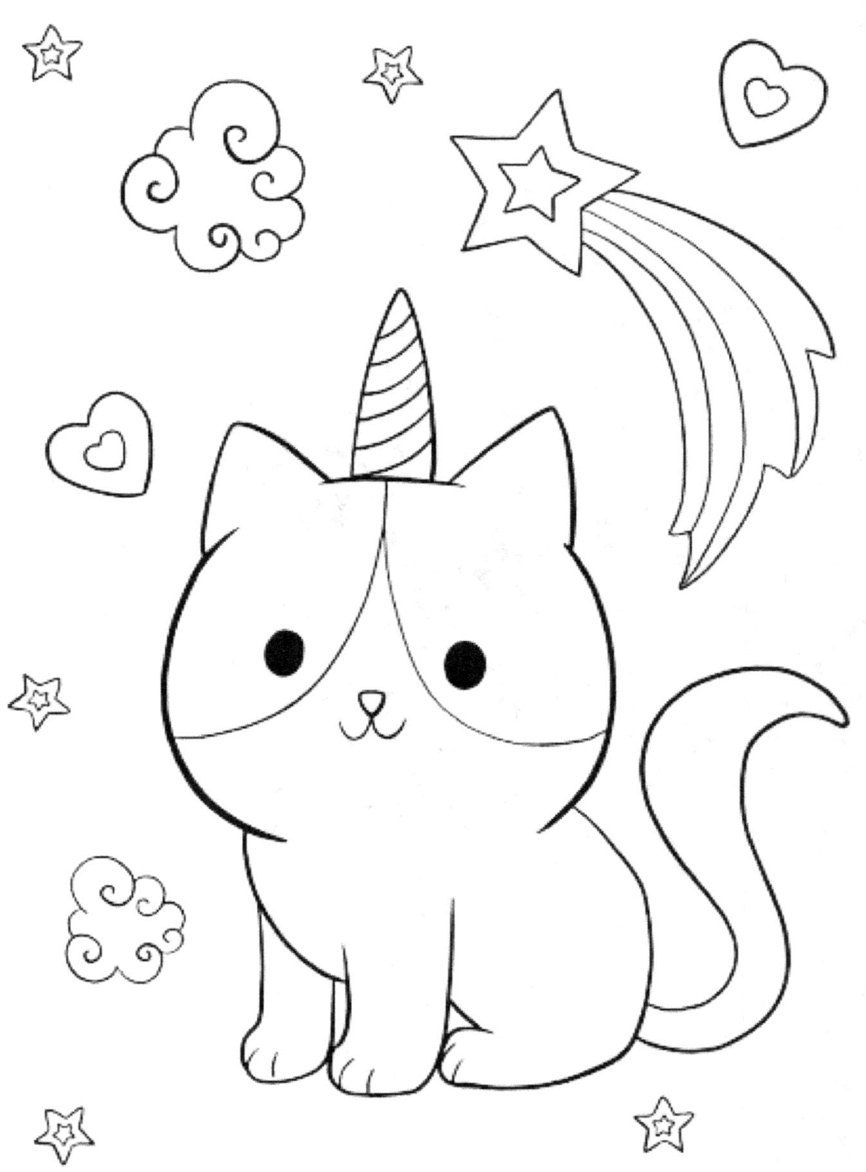

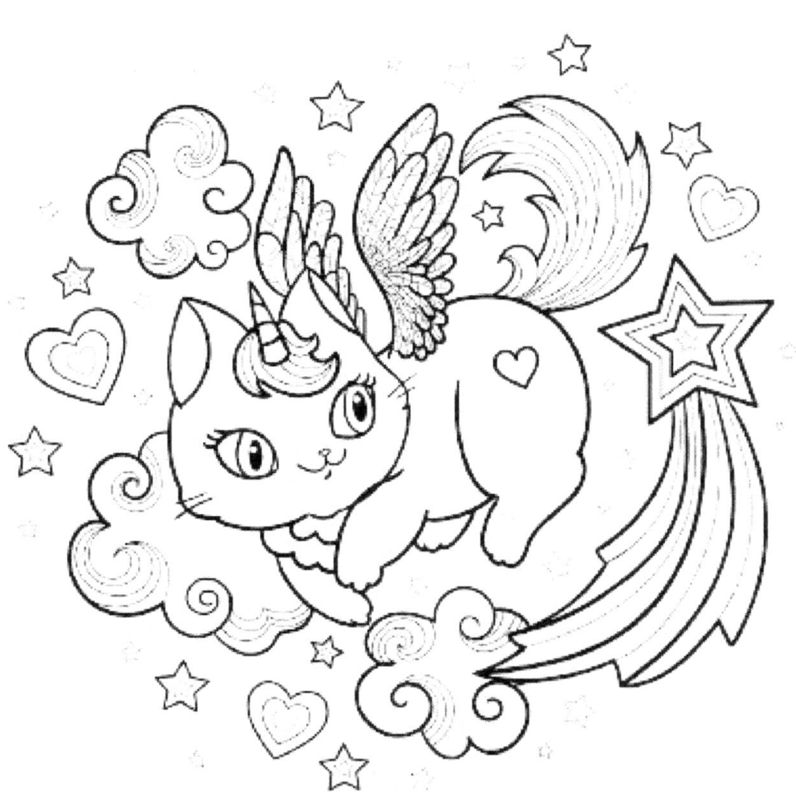

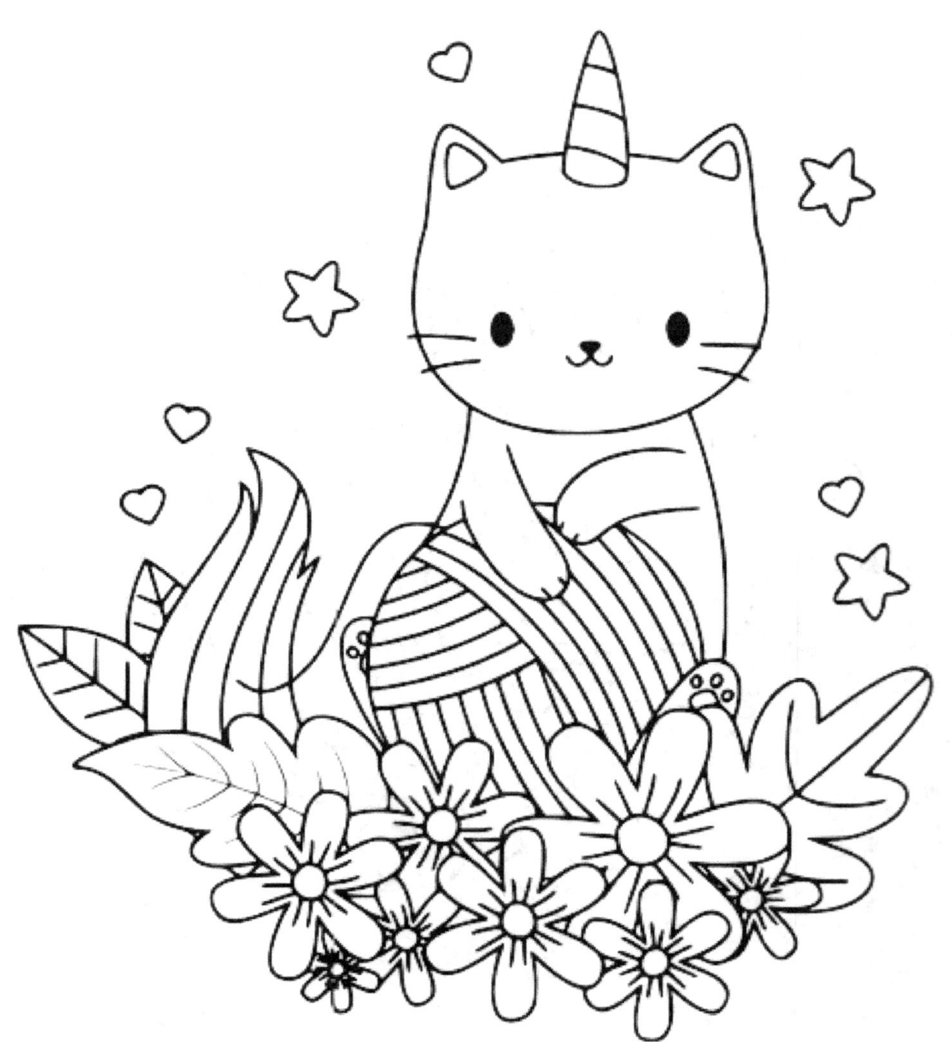

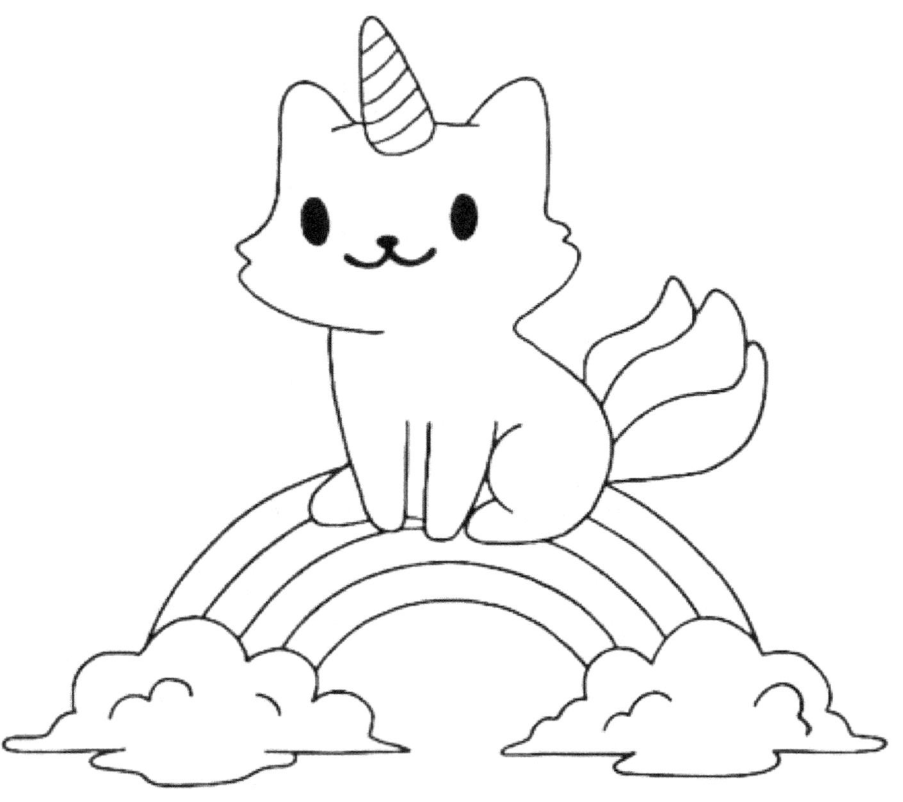

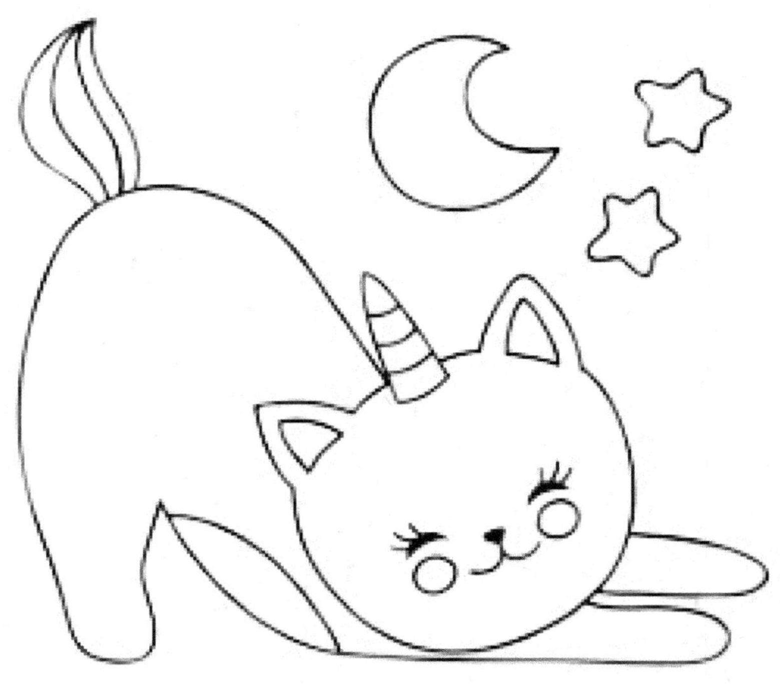

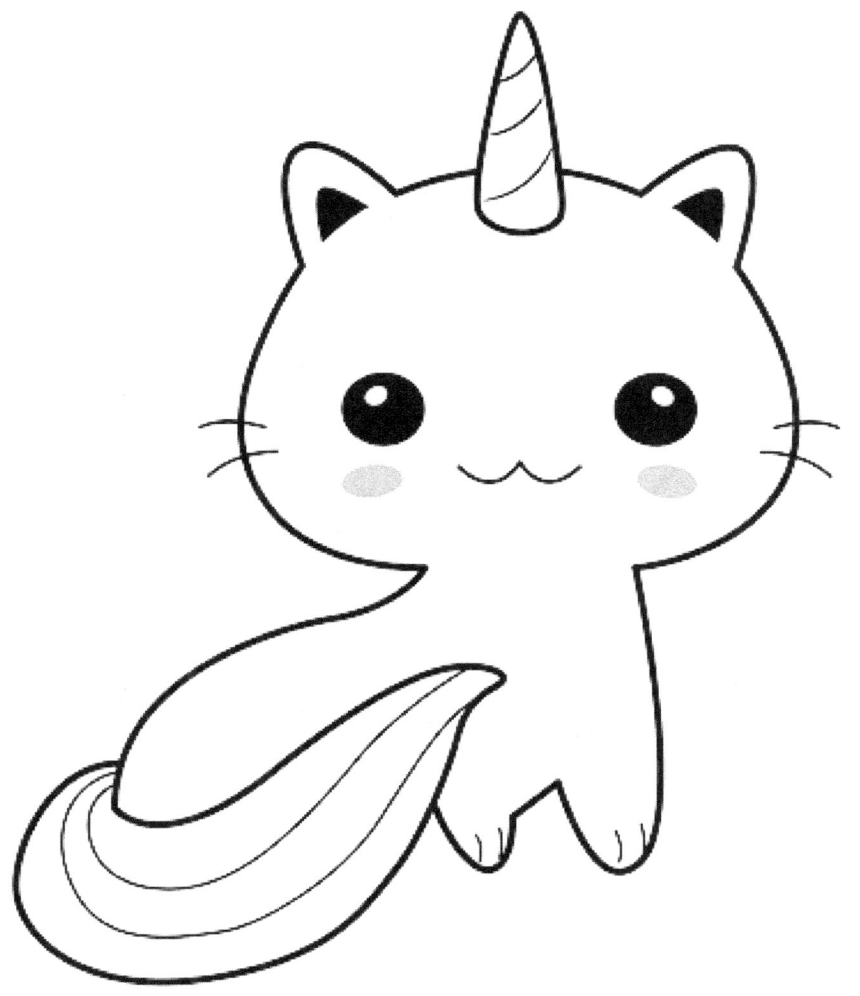

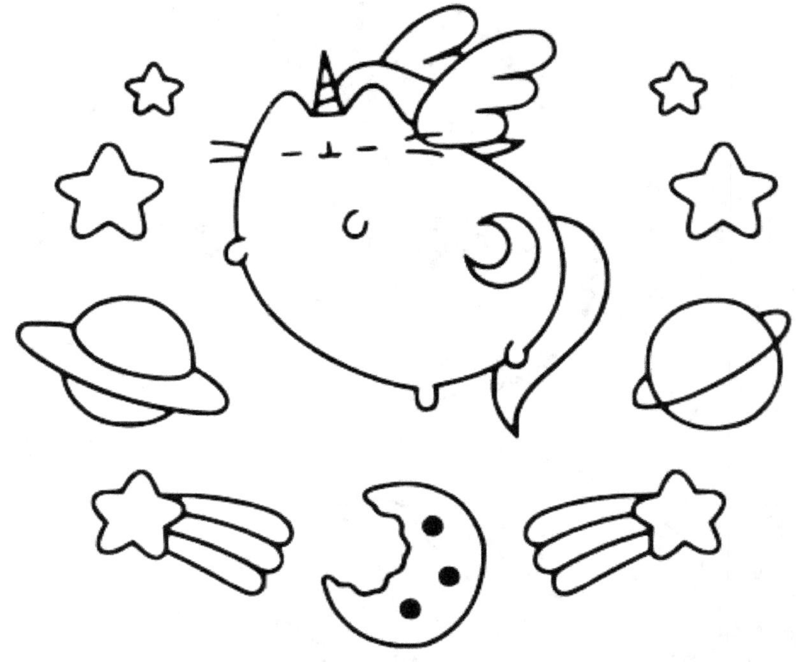

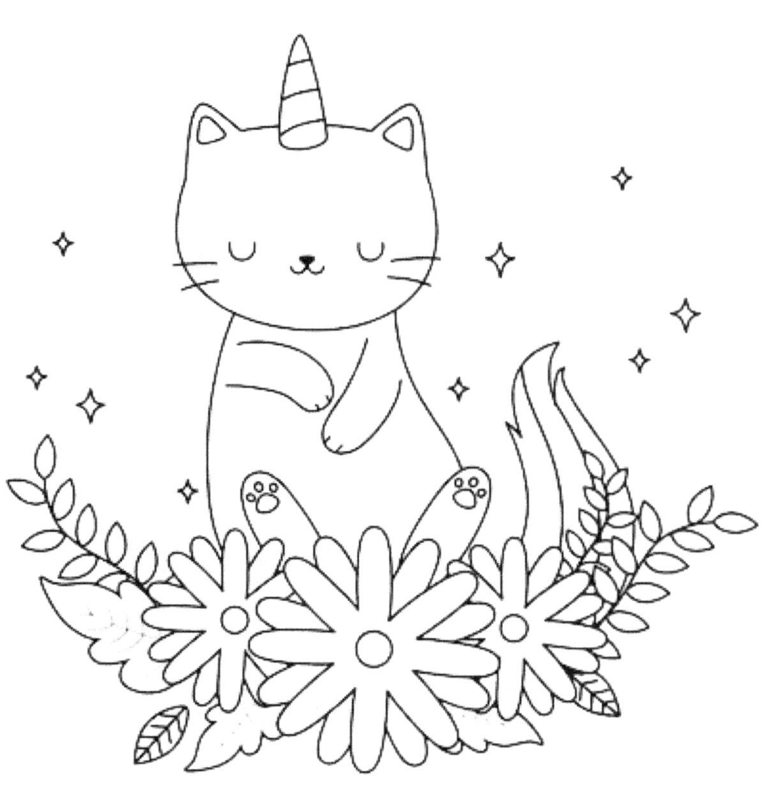

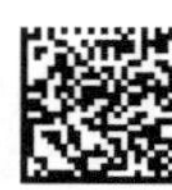

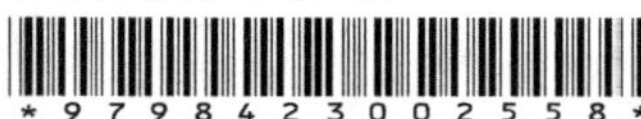